[illegible]

R.W. Younkin

CHRISTIANITY

AND MODERN THOUGHT

CHRISTIANITY AND MODERN THOUGHT

BY

CHARLES R. BROWN

CHARLES A. DINSMORE

RICHARD S. LULL

EDWARD G. SPAULDING

ALBERT P. FITCH

BENJAMIN W. BACON

WILLARD L. SPERRY

CHARLES W. GILKEY

ROBERT E. SPEER

EDITED WITH A FOREWORD BY

RALPH H. GABRIEL

NEW HAVEN · YALE UNIVERSITY PRESS

LONDON · HUMPHREY MILFORD · OXFORD UNIVERSITY PRESS

MCMXXIV

PRINTED IN THE UNITED STATES OF AMERICA

A FOREWORD

THEOLOGY on the front pages of the metropolitan press in 1923 and 1924 was both a novel and an unexpected American phenomenon. The United States has before been the scene of controversies within its churches, but it is doubtful if even the ecclesiastical dispute over slavery which broke in two some of the larger denominations drew the attention of the people as has the Fundamentalist Movement of the twentieth century. The popular reaction toward this struggle has badly shaken the theory of American indifference toward things of religion. Christianity, battered by recent world events, is displaying what to some is an unexpected vitality.

There are many folk who think that Christianity has outlived its usefulness. They feel that the great achievements of modern learning have antiquated the doctrines of the humble teacher of ancient Palestine and that frank agnosticism is the only sound foundation for an individual's philosophy of life. Their conviction is strengthened when they review the many instances in the past when the Church has openly opposed the advance of knowledge. There is also a group who hold that, in 1914, Christianity met its supreme test and failed. In that fateful year, with appalling suddenness, the forces of destruction which civilization had both begotten and chained were loosed, and the culture of Europe faced a danger greater than any since the barbarian invasions. The crisis found the Christian world sadly unprepared, split into different camps, the Greek, the Roman, and the Protestant churches. The last, in turn, was divided into a multitude of often picayune sects. The issue of the world conflict showed how far Christianity is from realizing its great ideal of universal brotherhood. Christian fought with Christian; and one group sought to bring the whole Mohammedan world to its aid.

It is true that, in the days when death was taking a terrible toll, the fundamental mysteries of life were brought home to people with unprecedented force. For a time the war caused men to think much on the problems of human duty and destiny. The spirit of a magnificent idealism was abroad, and there was a serious tone in human affairs. As the age-old mystery of death touched lives all over the western world, people flocked to the churches for explanation and comfort. Religious leaders leaped to the hasty conclusion that the fires of war were refining the dross from human nature and that Christianity was about to enter its day of greatness. They forgot that the war had also loosed passions which society only with the greatest of difficulty had brought under control. Such a loss outweighed any gain. When open war was succeeded by a hollow peace, the tragedy of the dominant religion of the West came clearly into view.

America had been unified by the World War as never before in her history. While the glory of the great illusion still shone in the land, her Protestant leaders thought the time propitious for the gathering of her religious forces into a common enterprise that would make of American Christianity a beacon lighting the whole world. The Inter-Church World Movement was a splendid conception. Behind it lay all the knowledge about organization and propaganda that the war had brought into being. Within the hearts of its leaders burned the fires of a great purpose. The day of petty sectarianism seemed at an end. As the armies of the Allies had been united to crush the monster, militarism, so the armies of Protestantism should be united to make war on the powers of darkness. Yet the Inter-Church World Movement collapsed with a dismaying suddenness, probably the most spectacular failure of Christianity in the new world. In less than a decade after its fall American Protestantism faces its most threatening schism. The new fight centers about the Bible.

The Church of the twentieth century confronts a new set of conditions. Eighteenth and nineteenth century scholarship has borne fruit and the mass of knowledge which it has accumulated is a most important part of the foundation of modern civilization. The superstructure of our culture has been rebuilt in adjustment to the new learning. The Church has been no exception; like every other human institution it has been compelled to adapt itself to the intellectual development of the last two centuries. Its first reactions of hostility resulted in defeat. Then Protestantism demonstrated its inherent strength. In a quiet way the results of the new scholarship were brought into religious thinking and became a part of its structure. More and more the method and the point of view of the new investigator began to shape the work of the leaders in religious thought. There is no such thing as sectarianism in the scholar's search for truth. Differences of opinion appear, but they do not affect the fundamental principle that every statement or hypothesis must be tested by the facts and must run the gauntlet of the severest criticism. Such an attitude is the antithesis of the denominationalism which teaches that the kingdom of heaven can only be achieved by a certain formula and that other opinions are unfortunate error. The Church itself applied the critical method to the investigation of that body of writings grouped together in the Bible and undertook the difficult and still unfinished task of separating the chaff from the wheat. Criticism quickly made it clear that the old doctrine of literal Biblical interpretation would have to be modified.

Many people, therefore, have been surprised at the sudden reappearance in the Fundamentalist Movement of this outgrown dogma. They forget a number of things about the Protestant churches which help in explaining the phenomenon. Protestantism, both in theory and in practice, is essentially democratic. Both its greatest strength and weakness come from this characteristic. Protestantism insists that every man, alone and without the mediation of a priest, shall face the mysteries of life—shall be the captain of his own soul. Such a position breeds in some a rugged faith and in others spiritual cowardice. There are many who shrink from the responsibility. To such folk the authority of supernatural revelation is indispensable.

Because church members govern the local organizations, Protestant church leaders cannot in their preaching be very far in advance of the thinking of their parishioners. This makes for slow progress. Furthermore, parishioners, like voters, are susceptible to demagogic appeals and, when conditions are right, can be herded into great crusades. The Fundamentalist Movement is a crusade to save the Bible. Back of it is the havoc of the war—not only bringing mourning into the homes of the people but making them ask how a good God could permit such a thing to come to pass. The question is not easy to answer and, very frequently, individual faith has been wrecked by storms of doubt. At such a time of crisis, it is inevitable that many people should seek the protection of authority. It is the easiest and most comforting way; and, it should be borne in mind, it is practically the only way for those less fortunate folk who have neither the training nor the capacity to wrestle with the intellectual problems of their generation. Protestants have no authority to which to turn except the Bible; so the old doctrine of literal interpretation has again raised its head.

But also behind the Fundamentalist Movement is the conservative traditionalism which has been the tendency of organized religion in all ages. Beliefs and rituals that have come down from the distant past acquire a sanctity that gives them a powerful grip on human life. They become the basis for elaborate ecclesiastical doctrines. If one of these foundation stones be struck from its place, there are many who believe the whole structure of faith must tumble in. So long as modern learning was largely confined to the colleges and universities and their small number of graduates, its repudiation of many of the doctrines of antiquity was little noticed by the public. But when, after the war, the youth of the nation began flooding the institutions of higher learning and the popularization of knowledge through outlines of science, history, literature, and art became almost a fad, the religious conceptions of a host of work-a-day Americans came suddenly into collision with the new learning. To many such people the Darwinian hypothesis seemed to drag men down to the level of the brute and criticism of the Bible to profane the Lord's handiwork. The old beliefs they knew and loved, but the new ideas seemed to destroy the very foundations of religion and to leave the individual forsaken in a Godless world. It was the instinct of self-preservation which raised from ocean to ocean a cry of fear from honest men and women who believed that all they held true and sacred was in jeopardy. Then a group of crusaders, both lay and ecclesiastical, dedicated their lives to the defence of Holy Writ.

Over against the halting and often perplexed modern seeker after truth they have put the Book of the Ages. With a splendid sincerity they have called to the minds of their countrymen the danger to their homes and institutions which must grow out of the decay of the old religion. Over the length and breadth of the land men and women have listened to the message and have taken heart. Such is the background of the development that threatens American Protestantism with schism. But, although the Fundamentalist controversy may leave behind it the scars of a rupture, its ultimate effect will probably be to benefit greatly the Protestant Church.

Conflict strengthens the ideas and positions of the opposing sides. The present struggle is not only demonstrating how far Protestantism has gone in its adaptations to modern knowledge, but is increasing and perfecting those adjustments. Liberal Protestant leaders find themselves under the necessity of defending the results of those very scholars whom, a little more than a half century ago, almost the whole Church was attacking. Moreover, they are doing it with enthusiasm and deep conviction. The rapprochement seems destined to have far-reaching, almost revolutionary consequences. This acceptance by the Protestant Church of both the knowledge and the method of scholarship has put it in harmony with the greatest modern factor that is making for progress. All too frequently in the past organized religion has served only to conserve the traditions of antiquity and to retard advance. It seems fairly clear that liberal Protestantism is shaking off this inherent tendency and is putting itself in the way to assume a new leadership in a new world. It is the problem of religion to deal with the adjustments of human life to the infinite mysteries. But religion must shape the tenets of its faith to accord with what is known and must subject them to the fiery ordeal of criticism. This the Church is already beginning to do; and the result seems destined to be Protestant unity.

Such unity will not be of organization. Experience has demonstrated that that is both impossible and undesirable. Democracy, which is at the foundation of Protestantism, gives its best results when it carries with it considerable local autonomy. It is desirable that a congregation should have a large share in the direction of its own affairs; it is also desirable that local churches should be united into national organizations which develop greater stability and amass larger resources. But to attempt to weld these national organizations into one super-church would be folly. Variation in form of worship and organization is both inevitable and advantageous; as well attempt to standardize men and women as to standardize Protestantism. But, if the leaders of the denominations have the scholar's open-minded attitude toward the search for truth, intellectual unity will supplement and complete that of the Christian spirit. The Fundamentalist Movement, which is greatly strengthening the bond between the religious and the non-religious thinker, is steadily pushing the Church in this direction. In one or two years it has accomplished what might otherwise have taken a decade.

For this reason the present controversy seems likely to be of the greatest significance in the development of Protestantism. Christianity was, in its inception, a lay development in which the leaders of the regular religious establishment played a negative and retarding part. A new enquiry was undertaken into the nature of human life and the problem of human destiny. The present trend in Protestantism seems to be a return to the spirit of those courageous and liberal-minded men who dared to break with Judaism, and who, after their own manner, sought truth wherever it might be found. If the passing of the Fundamentalists leaves thinkers within and without the Church engaged sympathetically in a common task, Christianity will have passed one of its greatest milestones. It will be well on the way to becoming a new faith out of which will have been refined those encumbering superstitions and doctrinal antagonisms which are the heritage of ignorance.

The purpose of the following chapters, which are the outgrowth of a course of lectures, organized by the Reverend Roy M. Houghton and given in the winter and spring of 1923 in New Haven, Connecticut, under the auspices of the Church of the Redeemer (Congregational), is to present the points of view of a group of representative men, both lay and ecclesiastical, concerning various problems which scholarship, within and without the Church, has brought into being.

Ralph H. Gabriel,
Assistant Professor of History,
Yale University.

CONTENTS

KEEPING THE FAITH

CHARLES R. BROWN

Dean of Yale Divinity School.

CHAPTER I

KEEPING THE FAITH

CHARLES R. BROWN

THERE was an old man once who was not just setting sail—he was coming into port for the last time, as the event proved, so far as earthly voyages went. He was busily engaged in writing a letter to a young man. The older man had visited all the countries which the young man had seen and many more besides. He had felt the throb of life, the urge of hot desire, the bite and sting of temptation as the young man was feeling it at that hour—then he had added further installments of valuable experience. He had gone through the year without missing a single month, spring, summer, autumn, and winter. Here away late in December he was summing up his whole philosophy of life for the benefit of one less experienced.

This is the substance of what he wrote: "Endure hardness as a good soldier of Jesus Christ." Submit to those disciplines which mean added efficiency. Not by dodging difficulties but by mastering them, do men attain.

"Watch in all things and make full proof of thy service." Keep your eyes open and your mind on your job if you would make your life an asset rather than a liability when society strikes a trial balance. "Stir up the gift of God which is in you"—discover and utilize that unrealized capacity you have for something higher and finer than these surface activities which oftentimes are no better than empty gestures.

"For I am now ready to be offered. The time of my departure is at hand. I have finished my course; I have fought a good fight and I have kept the faith."

Now what did he mean by keeping the faith? What does it mean for anyone to keep the faith? What happens when a man loses his faith? We sometimes hear devout fathers and mothers expressing reluctance about sending their sons to certain colleges for fear they may lose their faith. In these days of religious uncertainty, when the Fundamentalists on the one hand are impressing upon the minds of men a somewhat rigid, mechanical interpretation of the great spiritual verities and when some of the more liberal, open-minded men on the other side seem to be losing their grasp on the more vital factors in religious life, with a consequent loss of fervor and zest, it may be well to ask definitely how much is implied in keeping the faith.

Let me say four things about that process of keeping or of losing one's faith. First of all, keeping the faith does not mean thinking about things in general exactly as men thought about them in the fifteenth century or in the first. There was a time when all men believed that the earth was flat and that the blue sky arched above it like the lid of a butter dish. We know now that the earth is round and that it moves in its orbit through the infinite spaces of heaven and that all those stars and suns are worlds, many of them vastly greater than this earth of ours.

There was a time when if a man's children were sick or if his cow gave bloody milk, he decided that in all probability they had been "bewitched" by some unfriendly neighbor who possessed that devilish power. Eight words in the Bible caused the death of more than thirty thousand people. The eight words were these: "Thou shalt not suffer a witch to live." The serious-minded men of that day took the statement literally, and they proceeded to put it into execution by harrying the life out of certain peculiar old women on the ground that they were witches. It is only a hundred and fifty years since the last witch was put to death by civil process. To-day if anyone should undertake to have a witch put to death he would be sent to the insane asylum or to jail. We have moved away from a vast array of beliefs which have been disproved and outgrown.

The same process has been going on in religion. We have advanced by trial and rejection, proving all things, holding fast that which is good, putting the rest into the discard. If we had a full description of all the religious beliefs which have been outgrown it would fill the Encyclopedia Britannica. Why should not the world to-day be wiser religiously than it was yesterday? Why should not we move ahead with open minds, ready to know more to-morrow than we do to-day? Keeping the faith, then, does not mean thinking about things in general exactly as Methuselah did.

In the second place keeping the faith does not mean that a man believes exactly what he may have believed ten or twenty years ago. Here was the leading apostle of the Christian religion, who had kept the faith in right royal fashion, saying in one place that great changes had taken place in his own religious belief. "When I was a child I thought as a child, I spoke as a child, I understood as a child. But when I became a man I put away childish things. For now we see through a glass darkly, but then face to face. Now I know in part, but then I shall know even as I am known." He saw that, intellectually as well as morally, life is a process of forgetting the things which are behind and reaching for the things which are ahead, thus pressing toward the mark. No man who thinks can stand still like some lamp-post on the corner.

It is perfectly clear that there was change and progress in the views of Paul as expressed in his earlier and later letters. There was a time when he wrote to the Corinthians in scornful terms regarding marriage as being at best an unworthy concession to the flesh on the part of those who felt it better to marry than to suffer from uncontrollable desire. He insisted at that time that the celibate state was to be preferred—"He that is unmarried careth for the things of the Lord how he may please the Lord; and he that is married careth for the things of the world how he may please his wife." In his later letters Paul would have married life nothing less than sacramental, urging husbands to love their wives as Christ loved the Church. In his view of the second coming of Christ and in other matters of belief, he shows change and progress when we come to read his letters in chronological order.

When I was a child I thought as a child. We all did. It was the only way we could think at that stage of our development. I thought of God as a tall, elderly gentleman, with long white hair and beard, something like my grandfather, who was a very handsome old man. I thought of Him as standing yonder among the clouds, watching me, especially when I had been doing something wrong. I thought of the Bible as having been dictated to certain "sacred penmen of the Holy Ghost," as I once heard our minister call them. I thought that they wrote down exactly what they were told to write, so that there is here the infallible utterance of God from lid to lid. I thought of prayer as a kind of magical performance whereby if a man was sufficiently in earnest and was sure enough of himself, if he used the right words and was careful to close his prayer with some such phrase as "For Jesus' sake," he could get pretty much anything he chose. I thought of the future world as divided into two great camps, heaven and hell, one a place of unspeakable bliss and the other a place of unutterable and unending torment. I thought that at death each soul was sent to one of these two places to remain there for all eternity. When I was a child I thought as a child.

But when I became a man I put away pretty much all of that as Paul did, as almost all sensible men do. I did not do it all at once. It cannot be done in a hurry. You can change your clothes in ten minutes, but you cannot change your old beliefs in a vital way over night. No one can pass from one point in space to another without passing through all the intervening points in order. It was a long, patient process of growth, putting away childish conceptions, that I might enter into a more mature philosophy of life.

I learned to think of God as resident, immanent in all these mighty processes, heat, light, gravitation, electricity, the movement of the planets, the growth of plant life, the growth of animal life, the growth and progress of human life. These mighty processes express His power and purpose. They enfold us and bear us on, for in Him we live and move and are, as fish live in the sea. God is everywhere.

I learned to think of the Bible as containing truths which had been slowly wrought into the experiences of men chosen for their moral capacity and spiritual insight. They too met temptation, faced duty, bore their sorrows, and carried their burdens, and in doing it learned something about the nearness and the helpfulness of God. We have here the literary expression of that continuous and progressive revelation which God has been making of Himself through the best that these men saw and felt touching the divine presence.

I learned to think of prayer as communion, fellowship, coöperation between these finite spirits of ours and the Infinite Spirit of Him who is the Source and Summit of all being. He is working in us and for us to accomplish His good pleasure. When we pray we make it possible for Him to work to advantage.

I learned to think of the future life as the continuance of personal consciousness, a further opportunity for moral growth to be achieved by the fiery discipline of pain wherever we have been doing wrong, to be achieved in joyous satisfaction in so far as our wills have been brought into agreement with His perfect will. And I thought of this whole process as being held and directed by the one God and Father of us all, who is above all and through all and in us all. These various changes of belief did not mean that I had lost my faith —these changes of belief enabled me to keep my faith.

In the third place then, keeping one's faith means the maintenance of a certain mood and bearing toward the great spiritual verities. The Revised Version defines faith as the act of "giving substance to things hoped for." Here are certain claims, not on the face of them absurd or impossible, but not susceptible of immediate scientific demonstration. I may accept them as furnishing a good working hypothesis for human life. By my faith I give substance to them as things hoped for and begin to act accordingly.

Then they become more real by my attitude of faith as I utilize them in the hard tests of life and try them out. God, prayer, duty, redemption, the sense of eternal life already begun—they all become intensely real as we live by them. Faith is the mood, the bearing, the response of the soul, which first gives substance to them as things hoped for.

The whole structure of society rests upon that sort of faith. We cannot wait for scientific demonstration every time—we must act upon the balance of probabilities. The merchant entrusts a fortune to certain ships and then turns them over to the skill and fidelity of a few sea captains whom he scarcely knows by sight. The military commander stakes the outcome of a battle and the fate of his army upon the accuracy of a report made by a few scouts whom he has sent out to reconnoitre. I feel sick and go to the doctor. He examines me by methods which I do not understand and then writes something on a piece of paper which I cannot read. I take it to a drugstore and give it to a man I never saw before in my life. He takes it back somewhere out of sight and mixes up something in a bottle and tells me to take a teaspoonful of it three times a day.

Now I do not and cannot know as a matter of scientific demonstration that the doctor understood my case or that he wrote the right prescription. I do not know that the druggist filled the prescription correctly—for anything I know the stuff in that bottle may be rank poison and if I take it I may be dead in an hour. But I put my faith in the intelligence and fidelity of those men—I take my medicine and get well. Life could not go on if we were forever waiting for certainty. We walk by faith and not by sight—and religious faith is the readiness to act upon the intimations given to us by Him who is above all.

Someone has defined faith as "that faculty by which the vitality of one being passes over and becomes the possession of another." Here is a little child taken for the first time to a great city. He stands on Broadway, New York, frightened and bewildered by the noise, the rush, and the confusion of it all. If he were left alone he would be utterly overwhelmed by fear and distress.

But the child is with his father and as they make their way down Broadway hand in hand, the serene confidence of the father passes over and becomes serenity in the heart of the child. His faith in his father gives substance to the security he hopes for. So the faith of a private soldier in his general enables him to share in the courage and confidence of a great commander on the day of battle. So the Christian's faith in Christ becomes a bridge over which the spiritual energy of the Master passes and becomes vital in the heart of the disciple. In every such case it gives substance to the thing hoped for and thus becomes saving.

Now keeping the faith means to keep that mood and bearing however we may be compelled in the face of growing knowledge to modify many of our opinions. Your creeds as you grow older may not be so long. They may not have so many articles in them. The trimming and embroidery on them will be worn off here and there by the rub of life. The outward form of your faith will change and certain aspects of it may perish altogether, while the inward meaning and content of it is being renewed year by year. The few great, main things which you esteem vital will become all the more real as the years come and go. If you stand ready to adjust your life to the highest you see and feel and hope for, you will be keeping your faith magnificently.

It is this process, as Phillips Brooks once said, which makes the mature man's faith rich and warm and real. It is like the house in which a family has lived for many years. Here the children were born; here they were christened; here they played! Here the daughter stood in the glory of her young womanhood with the man of her choice by her side as they plighted their troth! Here we clung together when sorrow came and one was not. The old house is mellowed and enriched by all these sacred associations. It is another sort of place altogether from what it was when the paint and varnish were all fresh and everything was new and unworn. So the mature man's faith by the hard tests through which it has carried him, by the glad triumphs it has brought, by the way it has enabled him to face temptation and trial, grows warm and rich and real.

You may or may not be able to subscribe your name with intellectual honesty to the Nicene Creed, the Athanasian Creed, the Westminster Confession and all the other great statements of belief as certain men have done in days gone by. You may or may not be able to announce as your own certain opinions you once held touching a certain body of religious doctrine. But if you have kept that mood and bearing toward the sublime verities by which men live, and if you are able to answer back in terms of trust and obedience, of aspiration and high resolve, then you have kept the faith.

It would be difficult to speak too strongly of the value of that mood and bearing. The power of belief roots down into things unseen and eternal. It uncovers deeper sources of motive and stimulus. It offers more august sanctions for righteousness and more powerful deterrents from evil. It steadies and strengthens the will. It gives reach and grasp to the upward, outward, Godward thrust of a man's aspiration. It calls into action heart and imagination so that a man cries as did the apostle of old, "I know whom,"—not what—"whom I have believed and I am persuaded that He is able to keep that which I have committed unto Him." So the man walks on serene and undaunted, no matter what comes, by the power of his faith.

When we view the matter in this more intelligent way, we have no occasion to lament the passing of what some pious souls have called "The ages of faith." The day for certain forms of religious credulity has gone—I trust forever gone. But was there ever a time when so many people were sure of God, a Being wise, powerful, beneficent, the Ground and Source of all finite existence, "the Power not ourselves that makes for righteousness"!

Was there ever a time when so many people of all nations and kindreds and races and tongues looked up into the face of Jesus Christ and saw there the glory of the Eternal! Not merely a wise teacher, a lovely example, a powerful leader, but One who is Saviour, Redeemer, and Lord!

Was there ever a time when so many people, discarding the magic of prayer, believed nevertheless that it can change the hearts of men by its moral force and sweeten the whole world by its fragrance, binding it at last about the throne of God! Was there ever a time when so many people believed that in this body of literature called the Bible we have a veritable message from God to the souls of men, able to make us wise unto salvation and furnish us thoroughly for all good work!

Was there ever a time when so many people looked forward to the future world, not seeking to map it out into all the details of heaven and hell, but believing that personal consciousness does survive the shock of physical dissolution, believing in a future state of being which has been brought to light by the life and teaching, by the death and resurrection of Jesus Christ! And so long as great masses of thoughtful people maintain that mood and bearing, we are keeping the faith.

It has been my lot recently to come in contact with many ministers of the gospel who have grown old in service. Almost all of them who had heads on their shoulders and not merely places to wear their hats, had seen occasion many times to change their opinions touching some of the articles of belief. But they had kept the faith. They had boys' hearts under their old jackets. They had in their souls all the bubble and sparkle of youth. Their natural force was not abated. They loved to preach the good news and to strive for the souls of men, to give battle for the truth and to believe in the coming of the kingdom, as much as they ever did. And by that very mood and bearing they showed that in right royal fashion they too had kept the faith.

In the fourth place, where these readjustments are made aright, they bring a new sense of breadth and of vitality to our faith. How the very language of religious effort has changed within the memory of many who still are living. Where are those men who used to talk about "brands snatched from the burning," about a few souls "rescued from a sinking ship and gotten into the ark of safety"; about handfuls of meal carried aside to receive the sacred leaven of divine grace; about small groups of people gathered out of the world, into the cloister or the Church, that they might be saved; about chosen people and favored nations made wise and good by the grace of God leaving the huge pagan populations outside in darkness and sin?

Where are those people? They are all gone or fast going. You have to travel far afield to find them now. Yet it is only yesterday that the chief purpose of religion in the minds of many people seemed to be the recovery out of a lost world of that small portion of it which might be saved.

Look at the mood and bearing which are now in the ascendant! Men of faith are saying, We are not here to snatch brands from the burning—we are here to put out the fire of destructive evil and to make the world a safe place for all hands. We are not here to save a few lost souls from a sinking ship—we are here to make seaworthy the ship itself which carries all these sacred interests and to learn how to sail it on all the high seas of moral effort. We are here to put the leaven of new purpose boldly down into the entire mass of social and industrial, of educational and political relationships, that the whole lump of human life may be leavened. We are here not to get a few fortunate people out of the world into the Church but to get the Church itself, with all its saving principles and spirit, out into the world that the world itself may be redeemed. And everyone who is giving himself wisely and warmly to that vaster undertaking is keeping the faith in a broader way.

We have gone as yet only a short distance along this high road of spiritual effort. The kingdoms of this world, business and politics, education and recreation, have not by any means become kingdoms of our Lord and of His Christ. But does any man with eyes to see and a heart to understand, doubt but that we are headed right? The very fact that multitudes of clear-headed, honest-hearted men and women to-day are brave enough to undertake all that, brave enough to look up into the face of the infinite perfection of God and say, "Thy kingdom come; thy will be done on earth as it is in heaven," indicates that we have not lost our faith. We are the lineal descendants of those men of old who through faith wrought righteousness, subdued kingdoms, and turned back the forces of evil. We, like them, having obtained a good report by faith, have not yet received the promise—we are steadily looking for that better social order which hath foundations whose builder and maker is God.

Every man who grows outgrows. By your own enlarging faith you outgrow many of the opinions you once held just as you outgrew your clothes. The day came when the boy's knee breeches were too short in the legs and too narrow in their girth. You had to discard them and take upon you the garments of maturity. In like manner some of your early and faulty conceptions of religion showed their inadequacy to clothe the expanding life of the soul. They had to be let out—some of them you had to let go. The things you thought and said as a child had to be put aside to make room for a more mature philosophy of life. But in all these changes if you maintained the mood and bearing of trust and obedience, of aspiration and high resolve touching the highest you saw, then you have indeed kept the faith.

The final test is that of experience. Religion is like a stained glass window in a church. No matter how bright the day may be, you cannot see the beauty of it from the outside. Come in here! Come inside and look at it from within, then you will know. Look out upon life through the eyes of religious faith! Taste and see that the Lord is good, making proof of His claims by your own spiritual palate. Take His yoke upon you and learn of Him and you will find rest to your souls.

Let religion be judged as other great interests are judged, by its power to contribute to the full development of honored and joyous existence for our common humanity. "By their fruits ye shall know." It was the Master of all the higher values in life who proposed this pragmatic test, the test of experience, the ability or the inability of the thing under scrutiny to work out satisfactory results. By those tests we judge the claims of music, of art, of literature. We are content that religion should stand or fall by this same test, by its power to contribute to the well-rounded and satisfying development of human life.

We need not be troubled by many things as Martha was, cumbered with much serving or dancing attendance upon the thousand and one changes in theological opinion. One thing is needful in the last analysis, choose that good part which shall not be taken away! "Here is the last great certainty," as a great preacher once said to the men at Harvard, "be sure of God. By simple, loving worship, by continual moral obedience, by purifying yourself even as He is pure, creep close to Him, keep close to Him and in the end nothing can overthrow you."

When the British fleet was about to go into action at the Battle of Trafalgar, Lord Nelson said to an officer on the flagship, "Signal the fleet 'England confides that every man will do his duty.' "

The officer returned a moment later to say, "I have no signal for 'confides'—will not 'expects' do just as well?" Nelson consented but his own word held the finer meaning. England confided that every man would do his duty; and England's confidence reaching out from a thousand homes upon the land to those men upon the sea became a challenge to every man in that high and hard hour to do his best. England's faith as expressed in the words of her great commander gave substance to the thing she hoped for. The men responded—they did their duty and the victory was won.

Signal to every faculty in your command that you confide in each one to do its duty. That very attitude of soul will give substance to the thing you hope for and bring you off every field of moral struggle more than conqueror.

RELIGIOUS CERTAINTY IN AN AGE OF SCIENCE

CHARLES A. DINSMORE

Lecturer, Yale Divinity School. Author of "Life of Dante," "Atonement in Literature and Life," "New Light on Old Truth."

CHAPTER II

RELIGIOUS CERTAINTY IN AN AGE OF SCIENCE

CHARLES A. DINSMORE

IN front of the Art Museum in Boston is a bronze statue of extreme beauty and suggestiveness. It is the figure of an Indian, seated upon his pony, stretching out hands in prayer and adoration to the Great Spirit. Three orders of being are represented by the sculptor. There is the solid earth, inanimate, insensate. Upon it stands the pony, belonging to a higher order of existence. Made of the dust of the ground, in him is life. He can adjust himself to a physical environment. Yet the beauty of the sunset means nothing to him, nor do the glory of ideals disturb his contentment. The Indian is formed of the dust of the earth, and of living cells like the animal; but a spark disturbs his clod. In his breast there is the push of an impulse to which the pony is an utter stranger. He has yearnings and aspirations which reach above himself. He is aware of a relationship with a Power above, whom he conceives as a Great Spirit, not unlike himself—stronger, wiser, eternal—to whom his heart goes out in emotions of awe, reverence, adoration. In the dark breast of this primitive man there is a sense—imperfect, indeed, but real—of an order of values and forces which is lifted as far above the animal upon which he is astride as the animal is elevated in the scale of being above the earth.

The impulse which leads the savage to pray and to

worship a Spirit akin to himself is part of the furniture of human nature. It has manifested itself in every age and in every race. "You may find," says Plutarch, "communities without walls; without letters; without kings; without money; with no coinage; without acquaintance with theatres or gymnasia; but a community without holy rites, without a god, that uses not prayer; without sacrifice to win good or to avert evil—no man ever saw or will see." Religion begins in this response of man to what he conceives to be a supernatural Power or Powers, the response leads to an attitude, and the attitude results in experiences which involve the whole man—his thoughts, his emotions, his activities.

This religious impulse may be very feeble in some men, for we differ in our endowments. Some are blind to color and others are deaf to music, and yet the religious response is seldom lacking in a human bosom. The Great Mystery surrounds us all and all have some sense of it.

Is our religion at its best simply a majestic and consoling faith, born of our deep needs and unquenchable hopes, touching and vitalized by no reality, a brilliant dream which our imaginations have thrown against a dark and unreplying void? Or can we to-day in this age of science truly say with the holiest men of innumerable generations, "I know God"?

> Play no tricks with thy Soul, O Man,
> Let facts be facts, and life the thing it can.

That we are living in an age of science requires no demonstration. Its purpose is definite. It aims at nothing less than the mastery of nature by discovering and verifying its facts and setting them in their proper relationship. The genuine scientific spirit is thoroughly religious in its receptiveness; its subordination of self to the higher interests of truth and humanity; its integrity and reverence.

But science—I use the term in its popular sense—is strictly limited in its field of operations, and in the kind of knowledge it obtains. It deals only with phenomena and processes, it has absolutely nothing to say regarding the nature of ultimate realities. It has no answer to those insistent questions which we all put to ourselves in our deeper moments.

Now we are the inheritors of the faith of the fathers and of the achievements of science; to the finer spirit of each we wish to be obedient. We believe that we honor God when we welcome truth from every quarter. We eagerly accept every fact which science establishes. We cordially accept the scientific spirit and apply it unsparingly to our creeds, our Bible, our ecclesiastical traditions, to all the sources of authority. We wish to hold nothing that will not stand the strictest scrutiny.

Nevertheless, we must ask some questions which science does not answer. And so in a universe infinitely rich we seek other oracles, another order of reality.

"Besides the phenomena which address the senses," said John Tyndall, "there are laws and principles which do not address the senses at all but are spiritually discerned." This is true. The world in which we live has not only physical facts and forces, but also spiritual values which are charged with transforming energy. Poetry has affected human well-being as powerfully as Ford cars; the sighs of love have shaken men as perceptibly as the winds of heaven; "Before the saint,'' says Nietzsche, ''the strongest men in history have always bowed down reverently because they divine beyond his wretched appearance a superior force that will match itself against them.'' Professor Spaulding has said that the pressure of the particles of steam in a piston head is as real as the particles of steam. I would affirm that the spiritual energy which passes from the saint and conquers the will of a strong man is as real as the pressure of steam. The holiness of Jesus Christ has sent down through the centuries and over the world a transforming power as incontestable as the light of the sun. In memorable words Tyndall reminded his fellow scientists of the reality of a higher world of human interests: ''The world embraces not only a Newton, but a Shakespeare—not only a Boyle, but a Raphael—not only a Kant, but a Beethoven—not only a Darwin, but a Carlyle. Not in each of these, but in all, is human nature whole. They are not opposed, but supplementary—not mutually exclusive, but reconcilable. . . . And if, unsatisfied with them all, the human mind, with the yearning of a pilgrim for his distant home, will still turn to the Mystery from which it has emerged, seeking so to fashion it as to give unity to thought and faith; so long as this is done, not only without intolerance or bigotry of any kind, but with the enlightened recognition that ultimate fixity of conception is here unattainable, and that each succeeding age must be held free to fashion the mystery in accordance with its own needs—then, casting aside all the restrictions of Materialism, I would affirm this to be a field for the noblest exercise of what, in contrast with the *knowing* faculties, may be called the *creative* faculties of man. Here, however, I touch a theme too great for me to handle, but which will assuredly be handled by the loftiest minds, when you and I, like streaks of morning cloud, shall have melted into the infinite azure of the past."

These words are as rich in suggestiveness as they are beautiful. Mr. Tyndall recognizes that man instinctively reaches out beyond all beauty, goodness, and truth to that Reality of which they are expressions. He has religious needs which nothing but the Eternal can satisfy. This pilgrim yearning for home, men have called a thirst for God. "As the hart panteth after the water brooks, so panteth my soul after thee, O God." "We came forth from thee," exclaimed Augustine, "and our hearts are restless until they rest in thee." Out of the Deep we came, upon the Deep we live, and to the Deep we return; the Deep within calls to the Deep without. This profound yearning of our better natures for a refuge in the Highest is evidence of its existence. In a world where there is no water there would be no creature that thirsted. If there were no air, there would be no wings; an appetite indicates that there is something to satisfy it. Men would not hunger and thirst for God were there no home for the spirit.

Life is an adjustment of internal relations to external relations. We have physical life because we have power to adapt ourselves to a physical environment. We have spiritual life because our higher natures live in vital touch with an environment which fashions and sustains them. Our religious instincts are as much a part of our nature as our bodily appetites, and because of them we turn to what Mr. Tyndall calls the Mystery, but which we call the Eternal God, to find unity for our thought and faith. The energy which science recognizes, the beauty which is the soul of art, the righteousness which ethics declares, we inevitably unify in God, affirming that beauty, truth, goodness, are all expressions of God, the ultimate Reality. We turn to God because only in Him do we find the total meaning and value of life. We trust Him not according to our understanding, but according to our great need. "Trembling one, pursued by evil, dash thyself against the bosom of thy God," reads a Babylonian tablet four thousand years old, and in every age men have sought refuge in the Eternal. We are well aware that our conceptions of this God are entirely inadequate. We cannot throw the girdle of our thought about the uncreated. In the fullness of His being He is infinitely beyond the reach of our imagination. His ways are not our ways, nor His thoughts our thoughts.

Gilbert Murray, in his charming essay entitled *Religio Grammatici,* declares that the chief purpose of religion is to give liberty. "Man is imprisoned in the eternal present; and what we call a man's religion is to a great extent the thing which offers him a secret and permanent means of escape from that prison, a breaking of the prison walls which leaves him standing, of course still in the present, but in a present so enlarged and enfranchised that it becomes not a prison, but a free world." Religion gives men the power to overcome the world. It enables the believer to stand amid the hoarfrost and ashes, the pain, the tragedy, the failures of life, not merely with stoical indifference, but with a deep peace in his heart and a shout of triumph on his lips.

Note the significance of this. Liberty, peace, joy, power, these are the permanent and loftiest aspirations of men. Liberty has been the banner under which the suffering ages have fought. It is the ideal toward which they have toiled. To be at peace with one's self and with one's environment is our dream of beatitude. To get power and joy men search earth and heaven. Yet those who have that quality which we recognize as religious have as an immediate possession those values which are the aspiration of the race and the noblest goal of history. The religious mind has this instant possession because it conceives itself intersphered with Something higher than itself upon which it can repose with confidence, and from which comes spiritual vitality.

There are three orders of human interest; the physical world with which science deals, the world of beauty and goodness recognized by art and ethics, and the world of religion which interprets them all and then goes on to affirm an Unseen Helper who aids us in our attainment of beauty and goodness. The difference between the world of ethical values and religion is the difference between the seventh and eighth chapters of the Epistle to the Romans. Paul had a vivid appreciation of the realities of the moral ideal and he aspired to reach it, but the power was lacking. The good that he would do he could not, and the evil he hated, that he did. "O wretched man that I am, who shall deliver me from the body of this death?" Religion is the perception and the experience of Another, like us, above us, within us, reinforcing our defeated wills and giving us the victory.

Can we have certainty of this Other, this Unseen Friend, comparable to the certainty which science has of the material with which it works? What I wish to establish is the fact that a portion of our majestic faith grows into certainty, and certainty rests upon such evidence that it becomes knowledge as real as science possesses and of a higher rank.

Let us start with a clear definition of certainty and knowledge. Certainty is an assured conviction that something is so and not otherwise. It is entirely subjective and may be an illusion. Knowledge is to have assurance upon proper evidence that our mental perceptions and apprehensions agree with reality. Subjectively there is certainty, objectively there is reality, the connecting link is proper evidence that the inner persuasion tallies with the outer reality. We are willing to grant that the scientists have knowledge; but it is knowledge of a limited kind, knowledge of phenomena and processes, not of ultimate realities, nor of meanings.

There is a moral order which we know with the same certainty that we know the physical. Huxley, in a letter to Charles Kingsley, said: "The more I know intimately the lives of other men (to say nothing of my own) the more obvious is it to me that the wicked *does not* flourish nor is the righteous punished. The Ledger of the Almighty is strictly kept, and every one of us has the balance of his operations paid over to him at the end of every minute of his existence. . . . The absolute justice of the system of things is as clear to me as any scientific fact. The gravitation of sin to sorrow is as certain as that of the earth to the sun, and more so—for experimental proof of the fact is within reach of us all—nay is before us all in our lives, if we had but the eyes to see it." The knowledge we have of ethical values and laws is not the same kind of knowledge which we have of physical facts and laws, but it is valid knowledge. The evidences differ and are arrived at by different methods of procedure, but the results are equally indubitable.

Have we knowledge of the concern of religion? Both science and religion begin with an act of faith. Science trusts the general credibility of the sense perceptions and the conclusions of the understanding, religion trusts the intuitions and the emotions of man's higher nature. Both assume a Something external to the mind of man. The scientist, when he speaks of it, calls it power or energy; the religious man calls it God. The method of science is experiment, the method of religion is experience. It appeals to life, the whole of life, and life under all conditions. Its knowledge is the experience of humanity throughout the full range of history.

What are a few of the facts and truths which we have learned? We know as well as we know our own existence and in every act of our existence a Power not ourselves. That Power streaming through our physical nature gives us physical life and its laws; that Power streaming through our higher natures sets for us ideals of transcendent excellence. These ideals of moral worth did not spring out of the dust of the earth, they did not originate in experience, they transcend it.

> In man's self arise
> August anticipations, symbols, types
> Of a dim splendor ever on before.

Working within us is the push of a Power to participate in these ideals of supreme value. We needs must love the highest when we see it, and loving we are under constraint to obey. We know that within us and around us there is the urge of a Power that makes for righteousness. We know also that when we struggle for the supreme ideals we are sustained by ministries of help from the Unseen.

More than this, when a man seeks to coöperate with this Power that is working for righteousness, he finds that the latent energies of his nature are released. At the close of the War a governor of one of our states, addressing the returned soldiers, used these memorable words, "We welded ourselves to our duty as by fire, and there stole into our minds a supernal illumination, and into our hearts a mysterious strength." This experience is ever reproduced in all who weld themselves as by fire to duty, to truth, to beauty, to righteousness. The illumination and the mysterious strength never fail. "I considered myself," said John Milton, when he threw himself into the struggle for English liberty, "a member incorporate of that truth whereof I was persuaded." When one makes such a complete dedication of himself to truth his brain grows clear, his will strong, and something of the splendor of truth descends upon him.

The long experience of man goes to show that what we call the moral virtues—righteousness and goodness in all their forms—have survival value. They conform to the Nature of Things. When man battles for them he is not struggling in a vacuum, he is sustained. He finds the Other in nature coöperating with him.

But, it may be objected, the argument that God is righteous and good because there are moral forces in the world is a two-edged sword. Evil and ugliness are also here, and most potent forces are they. True. But the universe is not indifferent. Two streams flow forth from the central Fountain of Power. One is good, and the other is evil, and we should be hopelessly puzzled as to the nature of the fountain, did not a third stream go with them—the conviction that the good is superior to the evil. We are so constituted that we are convinced that the good is better both in value and power. We find that evil is self-destroying, the good is self-sustaining. "The evil that men do," said Mark Antony, "lives after them. The good is oft interred with their bones." It may seem so for a day, or a generation, but it is not true ultimately. The evil that made Rome a cesspool has been absorbed in the earth. The poetry, the oratory, the justice, the heroism of Rome, are still a beneficent force. The evils which destroyed Athens have gone glimmering into oblivion; the beauty of her temples, the wisdom of her philosophers, the insight of her poets, are part of the wealth of to-day.

> Only the virtues of the just
> Smell sweet and blossom in their dust.

Not only does this Power not ourselves work for righteousness, but it works so earnestly that wherever evil appears and its true nature becomes apparent abundant forces are released for its destruction. Paul stated this truth long ago. "Where sin abounded grace did much more abound." Let an evident evil appear in any community or nation, and gradually there are liberated moral forces which subdue it and thus the world moves forward. The tides of the divine energy in man rise slowly, but they are as sure as the floods of ocean.

Another conspicuous truth has come out of human experience. Samson stated it in his famous riddle. "Out of the eater came forth meat, and out of the strong came forth sweetness." This world of ours is so constituted that good does come out of evil; weakness turns into strength, darkness is transmuted into light. Every sad experience of life is the raw material out of which the wise and valiant spirit of man can fashion wisdom, goodness, and moral heroism. "There is some soul of goodness in things evil," said Shakespeare, "would men observingly distil it out." This insight of our greatest poet is true. The valor of the moral will in man in its struggle for perfection finds latent in the grimmest facts, and streaming through the most unpropitious circumstances, a coöperating spiritual energy by which ugliness is turned into beauty and evil becomes the instrument of good.

This is our affirmation. God and the unseen world are not merely objects of surmise. We know them in experience. In the process of building character we have genuine knowledge of the forces which enter vitally into those characters. We experience and know a Power which makes for ideals of worth and sustains us in our struggle to attain them. We know many of the laws of the kingdom, and multitudes testify to the wonders of its consolations. Therefore we hold that the difference between science and religion is not the difference between knowledge and faith, between certitude and belief, but between two different kinds of knowledge. Each begins in an act of faith, each attains to its own peculiar knowledge, then each by giving substance to things not seen advances to further acquisition. One gains knowledge through the senses, the other through the heart and will. But there is this difference to be noted between scientific and religious knowledge. The scientist can verify his facts to competent minds by an experiment which is performed within a given time. But to prove that righteousness exalteth a nation requires the experience of many generations. Moreover, scientific knowledge is independent of the personal equation. A murderer can perform a chemical experiment as well as a saint. But religion is more personal. Its knowledge is conditioned on character. Only the pure in heart see God. Only the lover can know love; the doors of the kingdom are shut to the proud and the selfish. Our moods also have much to do with our apprehension of all spiritual values. We live on the border line of the physical and the spiritual. If we were wholly of the earth we should never dream of the higher realities. If we were wholly spiritual, we should never doubt them; but because we belong partly to the seen and partly to the Unseen, vision alternates with doubt. On these conditions we hold our knowledge. The perception of religious and ethical values and forces is so vitally influenced by our moral and spiritual condition that our certitude is sometimes shadowed. The stars still shine, but the clouds cover them, God seems to forsake us and the walls of the celestial city lose their lustre. This condition we recognize and take account of, as we do the mists which obscure the mountains, and the ebb and flow of the ocean.

As if to counterbalance this we find that religious knowledge is more intimate than scientific knowledge. The mathematician knows *about* his circles and angles; the musician knows much about music, but he also knows music. The lover does not know about love, he knows love; the saint tastes the very flavor of holiness. The scientist knows something about the forces with which he deals; the lover, the artist, the saint, know the quality of the values they apprehend. Thus religious apprehension seems to reach nearer the heart of the truth than scientific knowledge.

Science deals with the world out there beyond us. It knows only symbols of reality which are interpreted to the consciousness through the senses. But when we deal with what takes place in our own inner consciousness we send the shaft down deeper into reality. There if anywhere we touch reality in its completest sense. "By being religious," says Professor James, "we establish ourselves in possession of Ultimate Reality at the only point at which reality is given us to equal."

I dissent emphatically from Mr. Tyndall's statement that science employs the knowing faculties and religion the creative. By our imagination we indeed shape our conception of God, but we experience reality.

Beyond and above what we know stretches the majestic and glowing world of what we believe. Our faith may be severely rational, but it is not knowledge. This is not to disparage faith. To live greatly in this world one must root his nature in vast and tremendous beliefs. Out of faith came the songs of the world, and all high art, and thought. It is the eye of faith that sees the broad horizons, the color, and the gleam. Religion standing on the known experience of the race makes one bold and glorious affirmation. She asserts that this Power that makes for truth, for beauty, for goodness, is not less personal than we. This leap of faith is justified, because God cannot be less than the greatest of His works; the Cause must be adequate to the effect. When therefore we call God personal we have interpreted Him by the loftiest symbol we have. He may be infinitely more, He cannot be less. When we call God a spirit, we use the clearest lens we have to look at the Everlasting. As Herbert Spencer has so well said, "The choice is not between a personal God and some thing lower, but between a personal God and something higher."

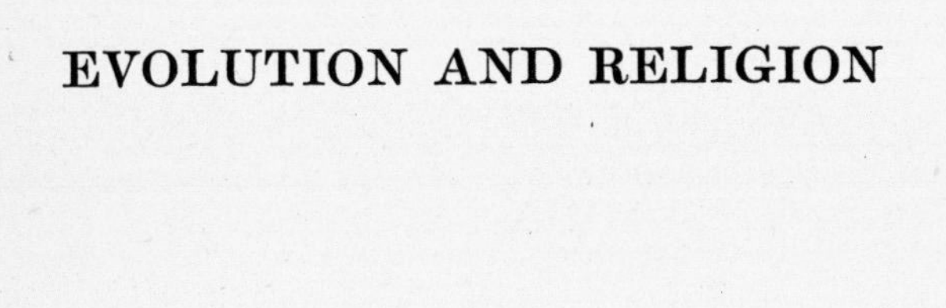

EVOLUTION AND RELIGION

RICHARD S. LULL

Professor Vertebrate Paleontology, Yale University. Director Peabody Museum. Author and editor of "The Evolution of the Earth and Its Inhabitants."

CHAPTER III

EVOLUTION AND RELIGION

RICHARD S. LULL

THE last year or two have witnessed a revival of the age-old warfare between science and religion, due in part to the emotionalism which invariably follows a great war, and in part to a misinterpretation of certain questions which have arisen within the ranks of science itself as to the causes of evolution, and which have been thought by the nonscientific to be evidences of disbelief in the doctrine of evolution itself. I wish, therefore, to tell you something of the development of the evolutionary idea, and of the extent and sureness of its acceptance as the only logical explanation of the phenomena of life.

The question of origins has been before the minds of men for thousands of years, and stories of creation appear in the sacred writings of many peoples, each one builded up of fragments from those which have gone before. Thus, from the Hebrew scripture comes what has been taught to many of us as the verbally inspired story, told with beautiful simplicity, as to a child, and sufficient to satisfy the minds of the primitive people whose sages penned the theme. But we are told by high authority (Clay) that back of the Mosaic account lies that in the Assyrian writings, certainly the prototype, and most surely the origin, of the Genesis story. Back of the Assyrian, in turn, lie other creation myths, all in the nature of folk-lore, handed down by word of mouth for thousands of years, and having their origin in the sombre shadows of prehistory.

I do not know in how far the priests of Israel insisted on the literal interpretation of the Mosaic story of the creation, and certainly among our Lord's recorded sayings there is no restatement of the theme, but the authorities of the Christian Church, despite the broader vision of certain of her disciples, such as Gregory of Nyssa and St. Augustine, became more and more insistent, until to doubt the verbal inspiration, and hence the literal interpretation, was to dare persecution or even death.

Father Suarez, a sixteenth-century Jesuit, was most rigid in his interpretation, and such was his influence upon the Roman Catholic followers of Europe that the story as he told it became the only orthodox belief for at least three hundred years, and for aught I know may yet be held to be. His statement, as quoted by Huxley, was as follows:

> The world was made in six natural days. On the first of these days the *materia prima* was made out of nothing, to receive afterwards those "substantial forms" which moulded it into the universe of things; on the third day, the ancestors of all living plants came into being, full-grown, perfect, and possessed of all the properties which now distinguish them; while, on the fifth and sixth days, the ancestors of all existing animals were similarly caused to exist in their complete and perfect state, by the infusion of their appropriate material substantial forms into the matter which had already been created. Finally, on the sixth day, the *anima rationalis*—that rational and immortal substantial form which is peculiar to man—was created out of nothing, and "breathed into" a mass of matter which, till then, was mere dust of the earth, and so man arose.

But the species man was represented by a solitary male individual, until the Creator took out one of his ribs and fashioned it into a female.

What Father Suarez did for Europe, John Milton did for Protestant England, not, however, through vested ecclesiastical authority, but because of the profound influence that his *Paradise Lost* had upon the English-speaking race. You remember his vivid picturing of the great creative movement in the sixth book—how the various brutes sprang full-formed from Mother Earth. So strong a hold had this epic upon the people that Huxley was accustomed to speak of the "Miltonic theory of creation" rather than of the Mosaic account.

The curious anomaly of the creation of light and darkness before the sun, moon, and stars, the manifest sources of light, disturbed none but a scientist, but the theologians themselves were somewhat at a loss to make the two accounts in the first and second chapters of Genesis agree, in that the former extends the creation over six days, while the latter seems to hold that the entire creation took place within a day. St. Thomas Aquinas reconciled the two accounts by stating his belief that the substance of things was created instantaneously, but that the separation and adorning took six days more.

The eighteenth century saw the rise of several great thinkers—philosophers and naturalists who were gifted with a clearer vision than were their predecessors. One notably, Carolus Linnaeus (1707-1778), a Swedish naturalist, although adhering to the special creation doctrine, nevertheless did much to stimulate zoölogical research by his masterly contributions to that science. He listed, described, and named with the double Latin names found in our present usage, some six thousand species in his *Systema Naturae,* which was published in 1735. Linnaeus did, however, in spite of his adhesion to the Mosaic doctrine, believe in certain post-creation changes. Thus, at the creation each genus represented a specially created type, but the several species of that type have been differentiated since, some by cross-breeding or hybridizing, others, as in certain parasitic forms, by degeneracy arising from their peculiar mode of life.

In addition to the increasing knowledge of recent animals, light was to come from another source of enquiry. A certain group of phenomena with which the writer is professionally concerned, namely, fossils, had been for a long time attracting the attention of divers men, although without any true appreciation of their significance. The ancients thought these objects to be merely the relics from some inundation, such as the Noachian deluge, or, according to the Greeks, the flood occurring during the time of Deucalion and Pyrrha; and that, although often found high on the hills surrounding the Mediterranean or Adriatic, they differed not at all from animals alive in the seas to-day. Yet others regarded fossils as the failures of a creative force within the earth, due no doubt to their occasional obscurity of appearance in the older rocks. Still others, those who pictured the creation as an actual manual labor of the Almighty, held the belief that these relics were models or patterns by means of which the more perfect living things were produced.

A fourth group held fossils to have been placed in the earth by Satan, either to mar the Creator's handiwork, or to tempt the unwary away from the strait and narrow path of revealed religion; while the prehistoric implements were regarded as the weapons of Satan's expulsion from Paradise.

From the theologians' standpoint, however, the most satisfying explanation of all was that fossils were formed for some inscrutable purpose of the Almighty. Thus they came to lie outside the pale of investigation, and this became the orthodox belief.

Leonardo da Vinci, whom most of us know as an inspired painter, was also an architect and engineer. While building canals in northern Italy, he became interested in the fossil shells which his workmen exhumed and brought to him for explanation, and he it was who first recognized them for what they were: the actual relics of bygone animals; and to this day the great amphitheater at Verona, begun under the reign of Diocletian in 290 A.D., and restored by Leonardo in the sixteenth century, has beautiful specimens of forms allied to the living pearly nautilus embedded in the rock-hewn seats.

In Paris during the time of Napoleon the Great there dwelt one of the most brilliant of French scientists, Baron Cuvier, favorite of the emperor, and a man of high scientific and social prestige. The founder of my own branch of science, comparative anatomy and vertebrate paleontology, Cuvier, because of his connection with the Sorbonne and the great natural history museum at the Jardin des Plantes, had the opportunity to become familiar at first hand with animals from all over the globe. Thus when bones were brought to light in the gypsum quarries of Montmartre, within the environs of the city of Paris itself, none was better fitted than he to pass judgment upon them. This he undertook to do, and upon comparing them with existing types, he soon realized that he was dealing with strange and unknown creatures which, while showing many points of analogy with living forms, were clearly not the same. But Cuvier was a special creationist, despite the fact that certain of his fellow savants held other views of animal and plant origins. Hence he advanced the theory of catastrophisms to account for the passing of these strange creatures, such as some devastating though local crustal disturbance and consequent incursion of the sea. He believed, if we interpret him aright, that a reëstablishment of previous conditions and a consequent withdrawal of the sea left that part of Europe again fitted for living inhabitants, the immediate ancestors of the present-day creatures. These he thought came from some other region untouched by the catastrophe, and represented forms in every way as much part of the original creation as were those which Nature had destroyed. This interpretation sufficed until geologists, delving in the older strata, found more and yet more primitive creatures, so that there were recognized no fewer than twenty-seven such faunas, each apparently separated from its immediate successor by some widespread death-dealing cause. However, Cuvier's method of repopulation by immigration did not suffice, so the creation belief was extended to include at least twenty-seven distinct creative acts, the last destructive agent being the biblical flood, which was survived by a selection of the antediluvial creatures through the divinely directed activity of Noah. The fact that this belief, advocated by the geologist D'Orbigny, thus drew upon the biblical narrative for its completion, gave it a certain acceptance by theologian and scientist as well, and thus it had the stamp of orthodoxy. But it pictures, not an omniscient Creator, but rather an experimentalist, somewhat inexperienced at first, whose products were crude and unfit to endure. These His wrath destroyed, and experiment succeeded experiment until the existing perfection was attained.

Over against the catastrophists arose another school, the uniformitarians, whose study of geological phenomena led them to deny all cataclysms, and to argue that the present-day forces—rain, frost, river and sea action, earthquake and volcanic activity—suffice to account for all the changes that the world has undergone, without periodic increase in intensity or violence; and that as the earth's surface has suffered gradual but continuous change, so organic life is in a continual state of extremely deliberate but corresponding alteration. That there were periods of relative quickening of both movements, as in times of climatic stress like the last glacial period, with a corresponding influence on life, there is no doubt, and in this way there is a certain measure of truth in the cataclysmic theory, but that there were successive re-creations all scientists to-day deny.

They believe, on the other hand, that life was formed but once, at least on earth, and that out of that single creation of one or very few forms all the varied and various organic beings, from the humblest to the mightiest, both plant and animal, now and in the past, have arisen. The process whereby this differentiation has been brought about we call an unfolding, or *evolution,* and we see in it the grand result of the interworkings of the laws of life and matter, but the source of those laws, and the complete understanding of them seem to lie beyond the ken of scientific research. This does not in the least forbid their investigation, as did the theologians with their ban of inscrutability, but holds merely that their complexity is such, and their time of origin so remote, that final solution, as the scientific mind solves problems, seems doubtful.

The belief in evolution is not new. In fact, it is older by far than the Christian era, for the Greeks, particularly Anaximander, Empedocles, and Aristotle, wrote much of nature, and seemed to recognize, not alone the continuity therein, but something of the processes which have given rise to organic change. The influence of the Church was such, however, that the light the ancients had was largely dimmed until the coming of the eighteenth-century naturalists to whom I have referred—Buffon, Erasmus Darwin, St. Hilaire, Lamarck, and later Charles Darwin—each one of whom contributed his share to the establishment of the evolutionary theory, although we do not always agree with their teaching. It was the great Darwin particularly who, by his most detailed and painstaking research, made general acceptance of the doctrine possible, for he founded his beliefs on such a varied host of observed facts that he gave to what had been up to his time a plausible theory, the status of a great natural law. About the fact of evolution there is to-day not the slightest doubt in the mind of any scientist, but Darwinism, which is not the same, but refers rather to certain causal factors advocated by Darwin himself, is not so widely accepted. The difference of opinion among scientific workers concerning these various factors has led the unscientific to infer a disagreement over the acceptance of the law of evolution itself, and has been used by the so-called antievolutionists as an argument that belief in the doctrine is wavering and may fail.

Many theologians of to-day agree with the scientists that this theory of the *potential creation*—for such organic evolution may be said to be—is the only logical conclusion to be drawn from the great array of observable facts within the range of each one's individual experience. Its acceptance, however, was gradual, as it certainly does not accord with the strictly interpreted Mosaic story. Several of our modern conceptions have had a similar history, among them that of the form of the universe and the movements of the earth and other celestial bodies, for while not so concisely told as was the creation story, nevertheless they are seemingly upheld by numerous scriptural passages, which combined seemed abundant justification for the older beliefs. Does not the Psalmist say the earth is fixed that it shall not be moved, and did not Joshua command the sun to stand still while he captured the stronghold of Canaan? Father Melchior Inchofer, S.J., wrote in 1631:

> The opinion of the earth's motion is of all heresies the most abominable, the most pernicious, the most scandalous; the immovability of the earth is thrice sacred; arguments against the immortality of the soul, the existence of God, and the incarnation should be tolerated sooner than an argument to prove that the earth moves.

The law of earth movement was finally established by Copernicus and Galileo, the latter by his telescope in 1616. He was, however, forced to recant in 1633, when his resistance was weakened by age, and his confession was sent abroad as a warning to philosophers and mathematicians. The final concession of the Church of Rome was not granted until 1829, and only in 1835 was the earth-movement condemnation omitted from the *Index.*

It was said of the establishment of the law of gravity that "Newton removed God from his universe and put a law in His place," not realizing that the law of gravity is a law of God. So it is with evolution, and, as these other great truths have been established despite the most influential opposition, so this must surely be.

Certain antievolution leaders would permit us to teach the evolution of lower forms of life if we leave man out of consideration. This, however, is an utterly illogical thing to do. Physical man is as surely the result of evolutionary laws as are any of his fellow creatures, for although he has probably been aloof from his nearest allies for a million or more years, he was not always so. He is one with the rest of animate creation, the product of precisely the same laws and processes.

Man's kinship with the rest of the animal kingdom is abundantly attested, and this is no new invention, for did not the Schoolmen speak of him as *animal rationale?* That he is one with them is shown in numerous ways, among the most significant of which is the sureness with which he can be placed in the classificatory scheme. As a back-boned animal, a mammal, a primate, there is no ambiguity about man as there often is among lower forms of life. His nearest relatives, the great or anthropoid apes, are strikingly similar, bone for bone, muscle for muscle, organ for organ, and these by a method of transplanting may actually be interchanged. The nervous systems differ in proportions, complexity, and size of brain—differences of degree, not of kind—and the functions are so similar that much of our knowledge of the workings of the human nervous system has been gained through experimentation on the apes. They have similar bodily ailments, are tormented by similar parasites, and a very subtle and ingenious blood-test, which, it is said, might be used for a second judgment of Solomon, points not only to relationship, but to a nearness of relationship between man and the gorilla and the orang far closer than between these apes and the lesser primates. Human development, including growth of body from a single minute cell, growth of mind, maturity, old age, and death, is similar to that of other animals. This developmental history of the individual is an accepted fact. Is it any more difficult to accept the approximately parallel evolution of the human race?

Several fossil human species have been discovered showing a definite gradation of change, in size, posture, limb proportions, form of skull and jaws and teeth, and of the enclosed brain, whose mental attributes are clearly indicated. These form a rapidly growing body of documentary evidence for man's evolution which, while subject to the criticism of willful disbelief, is nevertheless receiving greater and greater appreciation for what it is.

Mr. Bryan's text, *In His Image,* based upon a deep and widespread conviction that man was created in the physical image of his Maker, pictures God the Infinite in terms of a finite being. This we hold to be an irreverent conception, owing to the physical imperfections of the human mechanism. The famous physicist Helmholtz once said of the human eye: "If an optician sent it to me as an instrument, I should send it back with reproaches for his carelessness and demand the return of my money." Throughout the human body there are many structures, certain of which are of the nature of vestigial organs, which had a very valuable function in our ancestors, as they have to-day in distantly related forms, but which, if our interpretation of them be correct, are no longer of service, and in some instances, due to their proneness to disease, may be actually a menace to health or survival. These Drummond called the scaffolding left from the building of the body, and as such only are they understandable. It is impossible for one to imagine an all-wise Creator thus fashioning by direct creation so faulty a thing, and especially to conceive of its being an exact or even approximate copy of divine organization. Romanes, indeed, remarks that in creating man the Deity took most scrupulous pains to make him in the image of the beasts. That God can and did take a human form is manifest in the Incarnation. "Jesus, being in the form of God, . . . made himself of no reputation and took upon him the form of a servant and was made in the likeness of man; he humbled himself and became obedient unto death" (Philippians 2:5-8). Does not the creation of man in the image of God refer rather to man's spiritual nature than to his physical nature?

Evidences of human immortality are not directly forthcoming as a result of scientific investigation, for this has to do rather with observed fact concerning the physical universe and the conclusions to be drawn therefrom, than with the mystical side. It does not, on the other hand, disprove it, and so widespread an instinct lodged in the breast of every type of man, to the uttermost savage, becomes a very real thing. The reverential laying away of the dead, not alone by existing man, but by extinct species, some of whom practiced it twenty-five to forty thousand years ago, points to the immense antiquity of the belief, nor do I believe that this is the anterior limit, for the older fossil men are known thus far only from a few accidental or natural, not intentional, burials.

On the origin of the human soul science is also silent. Was it also the result of evolution? It may have been; or a divine awakening of an already evolved body, as when God "breathed into his nostrils the breath of life and man became a living soul" (Genesis 2:7). A splendid book, just published, *Man and the Attainment of Immortality,* by Professor J. Y. Simpson, who has succeeded Henry Drummond at the University of Edinburgh, discusses this problem from the scientific point of view.

The theistic evolutionist does not deny the Creator nor the creative act; he is concerned only with the method of creation, with "God's way of doing things," whether by direct or immediate creation, as the literal interpretation of Genesis seems to teach; or by experimental creation and repeated attempts to populate the earth, with cataclysmal destruction of organic life after each re-creation, until ultimately "God saw that it was good"; or by potential creation of matter and energy and the laws which govern their interactions, as a result of which there were:

1. A cosmic evolution of the heavenly bodies out of

chaos—millions of suns and their planetary systems, covering inconceivably vast realms of space. Neither of the two great theories of earth origin, the Laplacian nebular hypothesis and the aggregation theory of Chamberlin, is entirely satisfying.

2. A progressive evolution of the form and structure of the physical earth itself. Of this there is not the least doubt, and instead of theories to account for earth's surface changes, we have a record of facts, some of which (earth subsidence and elevation, deposition of sediments and erosion, earthquake and volcanic action) are matters of present-day observation.

3. An evolution of organic life on earth, based upon the plasticity and reactions of animals and plants under domestication, and the observed series of organisms and their orderly progression from lower to higher forms in the geologic past.

4. A culmination of organic evolution in modern man, based upon an abundantly attested array of facts derived from developmental history, comparative anatomy, and especially from paleontology. The known series of fossil men, associated, as they sometimes were, with animals which, like the mammoth, have entirely vanished from the earth, have an antiquity which vastly antedates the creation date of the older theologians. If I sought for the actual common ancestor of man and the anthropoids, I should go back at least as far again, for the human stock is very old.

The principle of continuity of creation seems to be the only logical conclusion to be drawn from the vast array of proved facts which have been revealed to us. To ignore these facts, and to try to revive worn-out and generally fantastic beliefs, all of which are merely man-made, will be in the end futile, for truth is mighty and will prevail.

Our opponents contend that the theistic evolutionists put God so far away as to make Him no longer a personal factor in our lives. We feel that this is not so, that the God of the evolutionist is an immanent God, and as such a much more continuous and potent factor in our lives than was the occasional wonder-working God of the older theology. As Drummond said: "If God appears periodically, he disappears periodically. If he comes on the scene at special crises, he is absent from the scene in the interval." Is the all-God or the occasional-God the nobler theory?

I do not see the so-called harmfulness of the evolution doctrine merely because it is not directly taught in the Bible, for the Bible says not one word of physics, of chemistry, of anatomy, or of geology, and it should not be taken as a text-book of science, but rather as a spiritual guide. The assumption that a lowly origin belittles man is hardly true, for his direct origin from the dust of the earth gives him no greater claim to dignity than does his triumphant emergence from the condition of his prehuman ancestors. Nor has belief in evolution anything to do with the spiritual-mindedness of the believer, for while there may not be relatively as many religious-minded scientists as there are of the nonscientific, it is due rather to habit of thought and the character of the scientific mind, which require tangible demonstration of facts for their acceptance. The scientist's whole life is a continual searching after truth, but there must be utter honesty, no jumping to conclusions, and no guesswork, or the scientific reputation is imperiled. It was this attitude of mind that led

Huxley to coin the word "agnostic" for an honest doubter whose lack of religious belief lay not in opposition, but merely in lack of satisfying proof. It is often more difficult for the scientific mind to accept a doctrine purely on faith, but I am sure that belief in a divine Author and Upholder of the universe is more widespread among my colleagues than is generally supposed, largely because their adhesion to outward religious form may not be so extensive. But the belief in evolution as the rational explanation of organic, including human, origins is entirely aside from religious conviction, and their so-called antagonism is largely imaginary. As Fosdick says: "The real enemies of the Christian faith are not the evolutionary biologists," but those who "insist on setting up artificial adhesions between Christianity and outgrown scientific opinions and proclaim that we can not have the one without the other," a revival of the fifteenth-century teachings of Peter Martyr, who said: "If a wrong opinion should obtain regarding the creation as described in Genesis, all the promises of Christ fall into nothing, and all of the life of our religion would be lost."

To quote, finally, President Pritchett of the Carnegie Foundation:

> The widespread influence of science in the last half-century—not alone in physical science, but in the development of historical criticism—has committed thinking men unreservedly to what is called the scientific method in dealing with all facts, all theories, all beliefs. This scientific method implies no new invention, but simply that truth must be sought with open mind, and that it must be followed fearlessly whithersoever it may lead, even though the path lie directly across the oldest traditions. The day when thinking men are willing to yield

their intellectual sincerity in obedience to authority or to tradition has gone by.

Under the leadership of this spirit scientific men have come into a faith concerning man and the universe in which he lives, not so precise or so detailed as the faith of tradition, but none the less a faith comforting and reassuring to a sincere mind. Behind all phenomena of a physical universe infinite in extent, whose existence goes back to a time limitless in duration, the man of science recognizes an infinite and eternal power, the author and sustainer of the universe, in whom we live and move and have our being. This universe he sees to be a universe of laws, although we are not always able to disentangle the expression of these laws from the complicated phenomena which their interaction brings about. The man of science rests secure in the faith that he lives in a universe sustained by an infinite power whose laws make for righteousness and progress. Such a man looks, therefore, hopefully and confidently not only upon the physical processes of nature but upon the progress of his own race. Rising out of a brute ancestry, he sees the race growing century by century in intelligence and moral power. He has faith, therefore, that He who through millions of years has brought us up—it may be slowly, painfully—will lead us gradually into a stronger, nobler life in this world. Science has faith in God and in human progress.

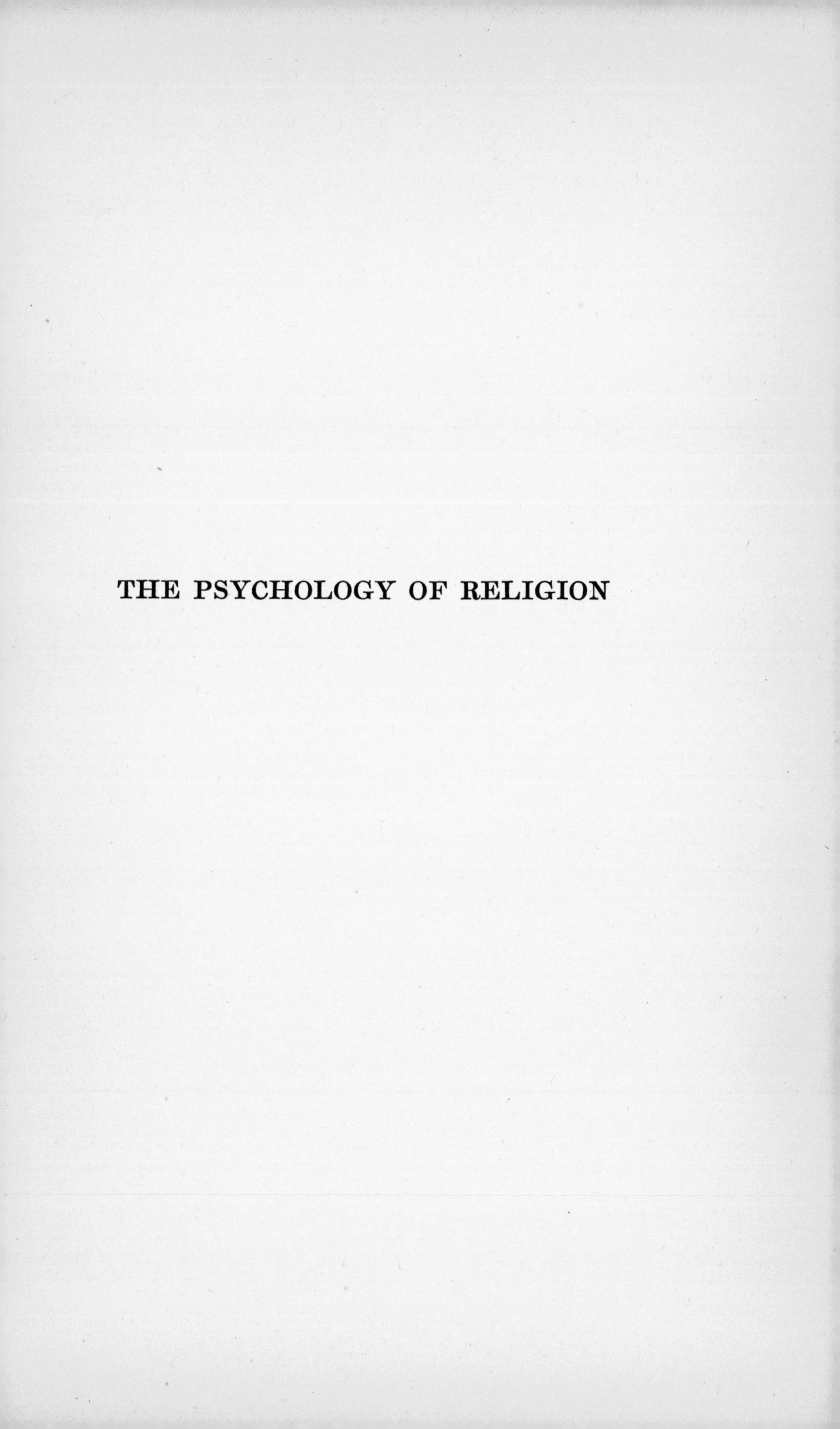

THE PSYCHOLOGY OF RELIGION

EDWARD G. SPAULDING

Professor of Philosophy in Princeton University. Author of "The New Rationalism." Lecturer at the Marine Biological Laboratory at Woods Hole.

CHAPTER IV

THE PSYCHOLOGY OF RELIGION

EDWARD G. SPAULDING

WHETHER one likes it or not, one has to admit that this age is in its thought preëminently scientific. If there is one characteristic that dominates our thinking at the present time it is science. Not all the periods of civilization have been scientific, as we all know. Science is relatively a modern thing, much younger than religion, much younger than theology.

Modern psychology claims to be a science, and although it is not as advanced as many other sciences, for example, mathematics and mechanics, it nevertheless does make good its claim. If, then, we are to take up the subject of the psychology of religion, this means that we are to look at religion from a scientific point of view, and that this special science, the psychology of religion, must be recognized as sharing the common characteristics of other sciences. There are many such common characteristics of science. Among the more important of these is the impersonal, unprejudiced, unbiased point of view—that point of view which means that one really does not prefer any one result to another as the outcome of investigation. If one remains true to this scientific point of view, as I conceive it, and studies the psychology of religion, then one would be as ready, for example, to acknowledge that all religion is superstition as to acknowledge the opposite—provided this were the conclusion to which the scientific study of religious phenomena led. The sciences endeavor to describe, to explain, and to learn specific relations of cause and effect, whereby in certain instances men can set up specific causes in order to get the specific effects they desire.

But if psychology is a science and shares with the other sciences such common characteristics, it is also distinct from the other sciences. It is different in that, as defined by William James, it studies consciousness as such. As defined by the modern behaviorist, Dr. Watson, it is the science of behavior—behavior being defined as what a living organism does when it is stimulated. Psychology, then, both shares the common characteristics of the other sciences, and yet is distinct from them, so that in the very special branch of the psychology of religion we must study either a very special kind of human consciousness or a very special kind of human behavior. My subject does not, however, commit me to the study exclusively of the psychology of the Christian religion. I shall discuss the psychology of religion in general.

Within the field of the sciences, one may approach problems either from the evolutionary point of view or from what is rather technically called the "factual" point of view; in other words, one may study things as they have developed or evolved, or one may examine and investigate things as one finds them at the present time. There is no doubt that evolution has come to stay, and that the general idea of evolution has already had the widest influence in every branch of knowledge. Indeed, the study of almost every subject is incomplete unless one pursues it, at least in part, from the evolutionary point of view. I shall adopt both points of view, the evolutionary and the factual, in what I have to present.

One of the first things to note in taking up the problem of the psychology of religion is the wide extent of the field. There is the psychology of prayer, of conversion, of revelation, or of ritual. I shall not select any of these special topics but rather consider that which I think is a very central phase of the psychology of religion, the belief in a Divine Being. But I also, as I analyze my subject, have to distinguish and keep separate religion in a rather narrow sense of the term, theology, morals, and the Church. Religion is primary. There would have been no Church and no theology, had not man in his native make-up been religious, whatever the source and character of that primary religious consciousness may have been.

I tentatively define religion, as distinct from theology, morals, and the Church, as a "tendency to reaction," by which I mean that there is something potential in human beings which prepares them to react in certain ways under certain circumstances. Or, to give another definition, religion is the conviction that there are in the general make-up of the universe one or more beings who determine men's destiny and who therefore bear a personal relation to men. In contrast with religion as thus defined, theologies are reasoned theories as to the nature of divine beings. Such theories are always influenced by the contemporaneous philosophy, science, and literature of the time in which any specific theology is developed. The Church in turn is an organization and an institution based on and incorporating in itself a specific theology and furthering the religious consciousness in individuals. Finally, morals may be defined as a code of conduct. While I do not deny that between these four there are the closest relations, nevertheless I should say, in reference to certain questions that have arisen in the United States within the last two or three years, that the conflict which some people think they discern is a conflict between science and special theologies, and not between science and religion.

The further examination of my problem shows me that, from the specifically psychological side, there are two points of view to be kept distinct. On the one hand I must consider the individual, since a religious consciousness and a religious attitude of mind is always in some individual living human being. But, on the other hand, there is also society, the crowd, the group, the congregation. The individual is made up of two classes of characteristics, those that are inherited, and those that are acquired. But immediately, again, I have to distinguish between two kinds of inherited characteristics, the one kind consisting of those that each one of us has inherited physiologically and mentally from our parents as they, in turn, inherited such characteristics from their parents, and the other kind consisting of those characteristics that come to us from society, not directly in the process of birth, but by instruction, imitation, and suggestion.

The individual is born with the ability to have sensations, to learn, to retain and to recall experiences, to perform certain instinctive acts, and to respond to suggestion. These abilities are, however, blank capacities. They are later filled in with a specific content, which, while the individual acquires it for himself, is nevertheless determined for him by tradition and the social environment into which he is born. Tradition, then, is that specific means of inheritance whereby at the present we are connected with the past,—indeed, with the more remote ages going indefinitely far into antiquity.

But the individual is not only an aggregate of characteristics which are inherited either from parents or from society; he is also shown by modern psychology to have both a consciousness and a subconsciousness.

There are various theories of "the subconscious." One theory identifies "the subconscious" wholly with that to which we are not attentive. Another theory, that of Dr. Morton Prince, states that subconsciousness is a co-consciousness existing side by side with our waking consciousness. A third theory makes the subconscious a lower degree or intensity of our waking consciousness, but continuous with it. Yet whatever hypothesis of the subconscious one may accept, all the evidence goes to show that the subconscious exists in some sense. It exists in the form of those past experiences that each of us has had, and has retained and can recall under certain conditions. For example, any person is not at any one time conscious of one-hundredth of the experiences of which he can be conscious. That of which he can be conscious and yet is not at a given moment conscious of, is in his subconsciousness. But the subconsciousness is organized. It is not the mere sum or aggregate of past experiences, but an organization around certain "centers." Thus there arise "complexes" or "mechanisms" with which there are connected certain primitive emotions such as anger or fear. Accordingly, these complexes or mechanisms are regarded by some of the psychoanalysts, especially by those who follow that very influential psychologist, Freud, as always identical with a wish or a desire which brooks no defeat.

Among the more important complexes is the "ego-complex," and growing out of this there are certain specific reactions which some writers on the psychology of religion regard as most important. Among these specific mechanisms or reactions are the following three: "the defense mechanism," "the compensation mechanism," and "the escape mechanism." As an illustration of the "compensation mechanism," the psychoanalyst of the present day cites the dreams of sleep and what we call daydreams. Each of these is the realization, often in symbolic form, of some desire or wish that is not gratified in, and that is perhaps suppressed during, waking consciousness. The "defense mechanism" may be defined as some kind of a device, often in very elaborate form, for the protection of one's ego, or of one's self-esteem. This may be illustrated by the case of a schoolboy who, being somewhat of a brag, has the conceit taken out of him by a sound thrashing, and who then, instead of bragging about himself, brags about his country or the United States Army. He thereby defends his ego from being injured.

The individual, then, is made up of two groups of characteristics, those that are inherited and those that are acquired. There is also in us a consciousness and a subconsciousness. However, those characteristics that are inherited, those that are acquired, consciousness and subconsciousness, are all organized into a unity that is the "personality." Personality is the result of, or is, indeed, identical with, this organization.

Into the individual, tradition may be said to enter through the fact that he is taught by his parents, by his teachers, and by his elders. The tradition is continued from one generation to the next and the individual receives it and is "made" by it, in part. But, also, the individual imitates his parents and those about him, and, finally, the individual is suggestible. Tradition thus pours into his subconsciousness, subsequently to well up into, or to produce its effects on, his consciousness.

Tradition is itself, however, very largely what the modern psychologists call a "crowd" phenomenon. Crowd psychology may be said to exist in two "dimensions," the one "dimension" being the immediate cross section of the crowd at the present time, and the other dimension going back into the past. In other words, history, with its traditions, is very largely a matter of what we call crowd psychology. Accordingly we must ask: What are some of the more important characteristics of the crowd? In answer we must say that individuals of a crowd, as opposed, for example, to an individual thinking by himself in his study, are always highly suggestible and imitative. Secondly, the individuals of a crowd are always very conservative in comparison to the individual, and oftentimes they are attached to something which they regard as sacred, this sacredness itself being very largely a product of the social group to which the individuals belong. Also, the crowd is very intolerant of all opposing opinions. There is further, in the crowd, a predominance of emotion as opposed to reason, and almost a total absence of inhibitions. Finally, the members of the crowd are like-minded, tending to think in very much the same way and to give attention to but one or to but few ideas.

Among the traditions which the individual inherits

is the religious tradition. Thus I may say that the religion of any person has to a very large extent been determined, not by himself, but by the fact that he was born perhaps in a particular nation and into a particular social heritage. In other words, our religion has never been a matter of our free choice, but is something that is given to us and determined for us.

This means, as Professor Robinson has pointed out in *The Mind in the Making,* that our minds are really to a very large extent, if not completely, "made." They are "made," on the one hand, by that which each one of us inherited as regards "mental" abilities and capacities from our parents, and, on the other hand, by the traditions that have poured into these blank capacities. That would seem to me to mean, then, whether one likes it or not, that one's personality, one's character, and the content of one's mind and character, are predetermined in a remorseless train of causes and effects, unless there is "some way out." And quite frankly, the only possible ways I can find of avoiding or limiting such a result are either, on the one hand, through sense experience, or, on the other hand, through reason.

I find, then, with Professor Robinson, that the mind is "made" by a twofold inheritance unless one can escape that inheritance by reasoning out things, and by using the information which comes from sense experience, as illustrated by the discoveries of science. But if the mind of the individual is the product of these two series of inheritances, and if there are, perhaps, very limited methods of escape from such inheritances, namely, by reason and by sensation, nevertheless, one must admit that individuals are not all alike in their religious temperament.

Professor Pratt, in his book on *The Religious Consciousness,* finds that religious temperaments are of four types. One type emphasizes tradition, and, therefore, ritual and the Church. There is a second type that prefers, as I would personally, to make religion compatible with reason, showing perhaps in that way, by submitting reason to its own test, that reason is limited, and that there is, therefore, ample opportunity for some kind of experience other than rational experience. There is a third type, to which Professor Ames of the University of Chicago belongs, that identifies religion with ethics and morals. And, finally, there is the fourth type of individuals, who, balancing things and finding no great advantage on either side, make up their minds to believe. They have "the will to believe."

Now, I dare say that the great majority of the readers of this chapter belong to the first two types of individuals, namely, those who, on the one hand, have inherited their religion from the tradition in which they have been brought up, but who, on the other hand, are quite willing to submit that traditional, inherited religion to the test of reason; who are quite willing to compare religion, theology, and the Church with the claims and criticism of science, and adjudicate the conflict. Wherever there are these two motives, there is, however, always the possibility of conflict, and if there is conflict, it must be resolved. But to resolve the conflict means that one must, perhaps, pull out of his subconsciousness into his consciousness those mechanisms that actuate him in what he believes in order that they may be submitted to the examination and test of reason in the light of as many facts as possible.

There is another branch of the psychology of religion to which at this point I would call attention. This concerns the question of the origin of religion. This problem is a difficult one because, perhaps, no one at the present time can find religion originating. Nevertheless, there are many data that give us much information on the question. These data indicate that there are possible a number of different origins of religion. Most of these origins have to do with certain instincts and primitive emotions, prominent among which is fear. Ribot and MacDougall think that religion originated in this way. What I wish to point out, however, in connection with this hypothesis, is that, if fear may be characterized as the primary religious experience, then out of this experience, at least according to some psychologists, there arose a "compensating mechanism," or a "defense reaction" that is religion. Thus, if fear was the original source of religion, not necessarily of Christianity, but of any religion whatever, there would be, as a specific reaction to that fear, a "defense mechanism" such as the belief in, and propitiation of, a Being who would be regarded as the means whereby one could escape from that which one fears.

Schleiermacher, on the other hand, supposed that all religion originated in a feeling of dependence, which would include, perhaps, what we call humility. But if this feeling was the original religious experience, then there may be said to arise out of it the specific "defense reaction," or the "compensating reaction," of conceiving and believing in One upon whom one is dependent, and in whom one can find the source of the greatness, the infinity, and the sublimity of things. Hope has also been suggested as the primary religious experience out of which religion has grown, and in this case there will arise the reaction of believing in a Being in whom one can hope and trust. Sympathy is likewise supposed to be one characteristic of the religious experience. Accordingly there will be the reaction of believing in One who responds, who loves. In the case of suffering, which oftentimes does lead people to have a religion, the reaction is the belief in a Great Alleviator. The impulse to self-preservation, or the "ego mechanism" itself, may lead to the specific "defense" or "compensation mechanism" of the belief in immortality; for the belief in immortality is a means whereby one defends oneself against the dislike of total destruction.

There are, then, these possible psychological origins of religion, or characteristics of the primary religious experience. Yet, in these various possible origins or characteristics of the religious experience, and of the reactions or beliefs to which they lead, there are certain common factors. The first of these is that every religious experience—I am making a distinction between religious experience and religious faith—leads to religious faith and belief. As a result of religious experience, men imagine and conceive, just as, because of certain experiences, desires, and wishes, they dream. This means that the evidence is that religion originated, in part at least, in imagination, with men unable to distinguish between what they imagined and what they perceived. The second common factor is that, in all of the reactions to these primary religious experiences, men hold to the reality and the objective character of that to which they direct their belief.

The third common factor is that every one of these reactions means that the individual holds to the real existence of something that is of value to him, of something that tends to make things better or even to make them good.

In the development of religion, both the Christian religion and other religions, all of these factors undoubtedly played their part, and, accordingly, a specific religious tradition has in each case developed which has always been to a very large extent a social phenomenon.

With such origins and with the fact of tradition, then, both admitted, I am forced to the conclusion that all of these original motives persist, and actually enter, to a less or greater degree, the mind of the individual who inherits his religion from the tradition in which he is brought up. In other words, I am compelled to conclude that the individual's religion is determined for him, unless he reasons. For it is only by reason that one can get a basis for religion that is independent of the tradition.

But this is not the whole story. In philosophy, at the present time, there are two positions with reference to the question of truth. One is that the actual development or history or evolution of an idea or theory makes that idea or theory true; in other words, it is maintained that genesis makes truth. For example, the question might be asked, with reference to legal principles, whether there is anything more to the so-called validity or truth of such principles than the fact that these principles have had a history and have worked successfully in human society to a greater or less degree. Opposed to this is the position that the truth or validity of a law or principle is quite independent of its history and development. The great majority of scientists tend to take this second position with reference to their science. Thus it would be said that, for example, the theory of Einstein is true, not because it has been preceded by other theories in the history of astronomy and now "works better" than its predecessors, but because at the present time certain facts are known that can only be explained on the basis of that theory. So we have the two positions, the one that genesis makes a "thing" true, and the other that truth is independent of genesis and history.

Now, although I cannot go into this question in detail, and can only express my own *credo,* I am personally of the conviction that the truth of anything is independent of its history, and accordingly that anything is true because it stands the tests on the one hand, of fact, and, on the other hand, of reason, or in a great many cases because it stands both of these tests.

Applying this position to the subject of the psychology of religion as I have treated it up to the present time, I find that, although the religious consciousness has had a development and a history, although in that development there has appeared Church and theology, and although the primitive sources of religion undoubtedly have persisted and enter the mind of each individual, nevertheless, at the present time, we can ask the question—quite fearlessly—whether religion can be justified in the face of all the facts that science advances.

My answer to this question is yes. But the further problem is how would this answer be justified. The way that I arrive at it myself is by examining the possible origins as well as the later characteristics of religion, and by finding in all of these the factor of *value,* of something that is of *worth* to the individual, or of something that means to him *betterment* and *goodness*. It is just this common factor that is present both in all of the possible origins of religion and in all the later developments, even, for example, in such a possible discussion as to whether one shall believe in a personal God or not. For, if one does believe in a personal God, then philosophically, logically, and psychologically, the reason why one so believes is because one finds that personality is better or higher in its presence than its absence; or if one believes in a Divine Being who is even above personality, that is, who is suprapersonal, then the reason why one thus believes is because one conceives such a Being to be higher than or better than a personal Divine Being.

Briefly, I find that science does not exhaust all the realities of life, but that we live not only in the presence of the realities of science, but also by love, charity, and justice, although I grant that there is not as much of these in life as I wish there were. Value or worth, to give a definition, is the common property or basis of comparison by virtue of which facts of experience can be said to be *good, better*, or *best*. Or, to state this in another way, in so far as I find that I do not and cannot say that one thing is heavier than another, or longer than another, or more costly than another, but that I can say that it is better than another, I am presupposing that there is, in this world in which I live, something of worth or value. That which is of worth or value may be an end in itself, or it may be merely a means to something else that is an ultimate end.

I can, then, in analyzing the psychology of religion, distinguish two things, namely, religious experience and religious faith. In religious experience we have fear, the feeling of dependence, hope, and the like, that are not identical with religious faith. There is also the experience of that which is good, of that which is of worth. However, that which is good or is of worth may be experienced as in conflict with evil. But the experience of such conflict leads to confidence and trust that, although the good in things may have opposition, it will nevertheless prevail. This is religious faith.

Accordingly, my definition of religion, not merely of Christianity, but of any religion whatever—for I firmly believe that other religions than Christianity have their truth also—is as follows: Religion is the experience of and faith in the presence in this universe of a principle of and power for goodness, between which and myself there is a very intimate relation. This principle is not material, not physical, and therefore it is not of the nature of those things with which the natural sciences deal. It is immaterial and spiritual. For the one characteristic that constitutes the nature of the spiritual is goodness. Indeed, goodness rather than consciousness, is, to my way of thinking, the fundamental characteristic of what I mean by the spiritual.

It is as if the world consisted of two kinds of reality. The one kind is dealt with by science, is measured and counted and weighed, and is, therefore, quantitative, while the other kind is not measured, but comes under the caption of "the good," and, in certain cases, the beautiful. The scientist seems to many to attack the existence of such a reality in our universe, but I think that an analysis of science will show that there is no difficulty in accepting such a scheme of things. Professor Russell, astronomer at Princeton, has stated that the nature of the mechanical sciences, from which so much opposition to religion is supposed to come, is very much misinterpreted. He illustrated the point by the example of the steam engine, in the cylinder of which the molecules of steam strike the piston head and exert pressure. Mechanical scientists sometimes interpret this to mean that the only realities that are present are the little particles of water which go back and forth with tremendous velocity and strike the piston head. Professor Russell repudiated this interpretation, and made the point that the pressure is just as real as the particles of water. To speak of the motion of these particles is, he insisted, only an hypothesis that is made in order to explain the pressure. In the case of human personality, although psychologists and physiologists can regard human beings as made up of atoms and molecules, of reflexes and instincts, and of subconsciousness and consciousness, there is also always a higher reality that is the *personality*. This peculiar reality belongs, now, to the realm of what I call worths or values.

Another point which Professor Russell has talked over with me in conversations that we have had concerning some recent scientific theories is that no science can get along merely by collecting sense data in the laboratory, but that every science sooner or later becomes a reasoned doctrine, and that it can become this only because of the presence in nature of something that is not material. In other words, there are immaterial relations among the physical or material facts with which science deals. Now, if one did not go any farther, this fact alone would indicate that there is the possibility of there being in the universe, in addition to the material facts with which the natural sciences deal, certain immaterial realities. Those immaterial entities need not, of course, be identical with what I have called "goodness" or "value," but if there are some immaterial entities, there may be others. So it is a question of fact as to whether or not we experience those other immaterial realities.

My answer is that we do. To me the world presents itself as a struggle between two factors, the one, the good, the other, evil; and my religious belief and faith consist in the fact that, although I cannot prove, I nevertheless am convinced, that the good will win out. It may be that the modern psychologist is right when he says to me, "That on your part is simply a 'defense reaction'; you are simply trying to rationalize that which you prefer to be true." However, the reply which I make to him is this, that I can study science as well as can he, that psychology is not alone to be considered in studying the problem, and that although there are undoubtedly psychological origins of religion, nevertheless these origins of religion are not its justification. The justification of religion lies in the fact that values are experienced, are as real as material facts. For example, I experience the beauty of a picture just as much as I experience the chemical constitution of its pigments.

In the general realm of values, however, I discover two kinds, the one positive, and the other negative; the one identical with good, and the other identical with evil. The question then arises, How should we deal with this problem of evil? In reply one must admit that there are various ways in which this problem has been answered in the past. One way is to take the position that we live in a world of mere appearances, and that behind that world there is a realm of reality. Evil can then be assigned to the realm of mere appearances. Another way is to maintain that evil is a means to an end. Still a third way makes evil an offset to the good, with the claim that there could be no such thing as good if there were not its opposite, evil.

With these different possible solutions of the problem, I am, however, not wholly in agreement. The scheme of things which I find I am forced to accept when I work out my own philosophy of religion is, that the Divine Being is not a creator, an architect, or a mechanist, in the sense of having started something going that has been going ever since. Nor is He a Being who reveals Himself to human beings, then to remain apart; but He is identical with the fact in the universe of *goodness* or of *worth.*

I admit that religious beliefs in their *origins* are largely identical with what the modern psychologist calls "compensation mechanisms," or "escape reactions," and that these mechanisms are the product of imagination and emotion. In the development of religion these "imaginings" are reasoned out in connection with certain ideas, so that the original emotions become highly idealized sentiments. A further "reasoning out" gives theological systems, and, as these theological systems are formed, specific ecclesiastical and religious traditions arise.

Each one of us socially inherits some one of these traditions. But the religion which one inherits socially is always open to examination by reason, and by criticism from the standpoint of science and from the examination of all the facts. Submitted, however, to such criticism, religion stands the test, although it may be that any specific system of theology may not have this good fortune. If this is the case it indicates that the fundamental thing in the question is, not theology, not the Church, but religion when this is defined as the acceptance in the universe of the presence of values or worths.

But it is also a psychological fact that individuals differ. There are the four temperaments to which I have referred, the rational, the ethical, the traditional, and the voluntaristic, the latter characterized by that which William James has called "the will to believe." With individuals thus differing, one cannot but conclude that creeds must also differ, as must theologies, and it is intolerance for one to maintain that there can be only one creed to which all should or could subscribe.

The Church is that institution which historically has maintained that there are in the universe values or worths. It is also that institution which historically has stood for the fight of evil by good. It is, accordingly, good psychology, in my opinion, as well as good ethics, to ally one's self with the Church.

THE FUNDAMENTAL BELIEFS OF CHRISTIANITY

ALBERT P. FITCH

Preacher, lecturer. Formerly Professor in Amherst College. Sometime Dean of Andover Theological Seminary. Author of "Can the Church Survive in the Changing Order?" and "Preaching and Paganism."

CHAPTER V

THE FUNDAMENTAL BELIEFS OF CHRISTIANITY

ALBERT P. FITCH

I THINK we would best begin by delimiting our subject. "Christianity," as we call it, is nearly two thousand years old. Like all venerable institutions, it is a rich complex; it has gathered a variety of oddly assorted associations with the passing years, absorbed many semiunrelated, mutually inconsistent ideas, rituals, and, even, practices. Indeed, with our present knowledge of its origins, Semitic, Hellenic, pagan, and of its evolution from these sources, in which, from time to time, it has conquered rival faiths by in large part absorbing them within its own movement, it is no longer possible to use accurately such a term as "Christianity," if we mean by that a clearly defined, self-consistent, and essentially unchanging body of belief. There is an important sense in which it is not true that there is any such thing as "the faith once delivered to the saints," although I hope to show, later, that there is another important sense in which that phrase is true.

One can speak of the Christian tradition, perhaps; and of the Christian spirit, certainly. But so far as there is any common denominator of the immense politico-ecclesiastical institution which we call the Church, and of the amorphous body of doctrine, primitive, Roman, Greek, Protestant, which all goes under the name of Christian, it is not found in a few intellectual convictions regarded as essential by all of them. It is found rather in a common emotion or spirit which runs, in varying strengths, through them all, and which, by its power, holds them more or less together. We discard, then, any discussion of common theological belief, since we should find small agreement here. The Greek Church would place first the Incarnation; the Roman Church, the Atonement; the Protestant Church of the moment, a variety of doctrines, chiefly, perhaps, Man, who is the candle of the Lord, the son of Man who stands upon His feet before divine Majesty.

Moreover, the classic doctrines of the Church not only have no universal acceptance, either as to the order of their importance or as to the precise nature of their content, but they are for the most part formulated in the ideology of an outmoded view of the world, and addressed in their practical application to the needs and defects of vanished orders of society. Thus, most men do not think, to-day, in terms of a dichotomized universe; we do not accept, either in philosophy or psychology, a fundamental dualism dividing the cosmos. Nor in our applications of beliefs ought we to address them to the problems of an ecclesiastical, a feudal, or an agricultural order of society, although it is in the terms of these vanished or vanishing orders that, for the most part, they are conceived of in their practical bearings. The initial mistake, then, would be to look for the fundamental beliefs of Christianity in any possible combination or selection of inherited theological statements.

But I said a moment ago that the one thing common to the "Christian" movement was a certain moral faith or spirit which has so vitalized its differing ecclesiastical institutions and its rival creedal formulations that they have all served as the actual vehicles of the religion of Jesus. That spirit has been their solvent and has even carried effectively an ever increasing ecclesiastical and theological impedimenta, drawn from ever widening and more varied sources. Our question, then, might be, What is this one thing which the whole Christian movement has in varying degrees held in common, which thing we call the Christian spirit or the Christian power? And what are the elements which compose it?

I think the first element in the Christian power is that it is summed up in terms of a person. There are some brilliant New Testament scholars, Mr. Kirsopp Lake in particular, who think we have overestimated the part played by the person of Jesus in primitive Christianity. The Pauline epistles seem to me to speak differently. Let us say then that the fundamental belief of the Christian is faith in the complete truth of a person, that Jesus, as the truth, is the heart of the Christian movement. But having made that statement, we ought carefully to guard and define it. Jesus was a man tempted at all points like as we are, molded by His social environment, even as we are, subject to the physical, the intellectual limitations of His age. In what sense can we say that all Christians believe, then, that they have found the truth in the person of Jesus?

Not in the historical sense. It is not essential to Christianity to see Him as the incarnation of historical truth. That is to say, it is beside the point whether every statement regarding external events, whether made by Him, or about Him, corresponds with fact. The infancy narratives, the dogma of the virgin birth, the resurrection story, may or may not be true. This is a question of factual evidence and not in it resides the secret of the Christian power. Nor is it essential to Christianity to regard Him as an incarnation of scientific truth. That is, it is beside the point whether or not all His ideas corresponded with reality. He appears to have believed that physical and mental disturbances were the result of demoniac possession, to have believed in a theory of the nature of the universe which before the days of Copernicus was generally accepted. These ideas may or may not have been true. That is a question of scientific investigation, and neither in belief nor disbelief in them is found the secret of the Christian power.

But I suppose the test comes when we say that all Christians believe in Jesus as the personification of moral and religious truth; that is, as one who found and lived truth in all His personal relationships. We get in Him the impression of a perfect correspondence between speech and thought, outward expression and inward conviction. In Him we find harmony of relationships, all that He ought to be in dealing with other people, whether as a son, a citizen, a friend, a social leader, a spiritual seer. We find in Him an essentially unbroken consciousness of the Divine Presence, and a perfectly achieved harmony with the Divine Will. It is that utter moral integrity which subdued His disciples to awe, and the record of which their followers transmitted in the Gospel, and which an elder world called, in theological terms, His sinlessness. In short, the first thing common to all Christians is that they have a personal leader whom they believe to have been an absolutely true person. And perhaps for mankind, truth, in the terms of a person, is the highest form of it.

Now if the heart of the Christian power is this sort of belief in Jesus, we can retrace our steps for a moment and again clear the ground of many misconceptions of what both its friends and its foes sometimes say is essential to Christianity. It is not fundamental to being a Christian to subscribe, or fail to subscribe, to any metaphysical speculation as to the divine or human nature of Jesus, or any metaphysical speculation as to the nature of God. It is not belief in a third person in a Trinity, or in a miracle-working prodigy, which has ever been the true and constant source of Christian power or is essential to Christianity, although it is often identified with these things. It is not fundamental to being a Christian that we should either accept, or refuse to accept, Jesus' world view, whatever it was, within which He worked out and formulated His message and lived His life. Let us assume, because at the moment the better part of New Testament scholarship does assume it, that He moved in the circle of the ideas of His Semitic inheritance. Let us say: The notion of development, of growth of the new out of existing organizations, was impossible to a man of His time and place. The idea, in other words, of the evolution of a new society was antecedently out of the question for Him. It did not exist, even in embryo, in His part of the ancient world. Hence "progress," as we understand the term, meant nothing to Him. Progress to Him was catastrophic change, a wiping of the slate clean, and the beginning over again of a new order. Let us say that He believed that there was about to appear another and a completed society, differing in kind from the then existing one, a holy city, a new Jerusalem, soon to descend from God out of heaven, and that He was the herald and would be the witness of it, returning again in glory on the clouds of heaven. In this belief, if He held it, He was disappointed; the new kingdom did not come; the evil custom of this world had its age-long way with Him; and, as regards these things, He died a disillusioned and anguished man.

All this may or may not be true. Personally, I think for substance, with some modifications, it probably is true. But again it is beside the point. It is not fundamental to believing in Jesus to enquire whether He did or did not know what history had in store, whether He read the movements of His time aright. For belief in Jesus as the personification of moral truth stands or falls with the intrinsic worth of what He taught or was in that realm, with what He believed and exemplified regarding human and divine relationships, irrespective of what were the occasions of that teaching or toward what immediate external ends, He thought it was moving.

Now we can begin to speak constructively. What is the first fundamental in the spirit of Christianity?

I. Belief in the ethical and religious supremacy of Jesus. The sign of the Christian is moral discipleship because the Christian power has been moral power, and the Christian spirit springs from moral allegiance. What Christianity means then by "faith" is moral trust. Faith in Jesus is believing what He said regarding the moral and religious nature of God and man. Faith in Him is confidence in that message, trust in His moral understanding, faith in His spiritual vision. What is fundamental to discipleship is the active loyalty of the will to His way of living and to His principles of conduct.

This includes, not as its beginning but as its consummation, His belief as to the character of God and adopting the appropriate attitude of man toward a Deity of such a character. So far as one can distinguish between two things that are interdependent, belief in Jesus would put as the beginning of discipleship the moral, not the religious. First, because He seems to have achieved, as He certainly summed up, religious understanding in and through ethical practice. Blessed are the pure in heart for they shall see God. It is character which brings insight, not insight which must be presupposed for character. So the first step in belief is doing as He did, believing in Him by imitating Him. They who will to do the will shall know of the doctrine. All over the world the Christian power has flowed from believing that what He said about the moral nature of God and man is true; what He did in His relationships with human spirits and with the Eternal Spirit was wise and right; what He condemned in such relationships is false. The principle of His life was right and I accept it. That is, I take it, the saving faith of Christianity.

We must not ignore the fact that this power and this saving trust have in large measure come down through the ages under the guise of a Divine Redeemer, a God who lived and died, and rose again, and whose supremacy in the moral and religious world was certified to man by the miracles of His Incarnation, and Atonement, and Resurrection, rather than by His intrinsic moral excellence, and who was regarded as having brought his saving moral energy and spiritual grace as part of a predestined world plan for the salvation of mankind. But what I have been trying to say earlier is that this old mode of thinking, this antique interpretation of the power, this assumed apparatus for its transmission and exercise, is not fundamental. And certainly it is not the way in which men either accept, understand, or are filled by the power, for the most part, in our world of this moment.

II. It becomes us then to enquire what is the content of this moral and religious teaching and practice of Jesus, the acceptance of which is the faith of the Christian. We may indeed reject it on the ground that it was meant for the kind of a world that does not exist. If we so reject it, then we cannot call ourselves, in any sense that could be called a universal sense, Christians. Or we may accept it on the ground that it sets forth a principle which could be workable in our world and the one principle potent enough to overcome our world. If we thus accept it, primarily because it appeals to our best judgment, we become Christians of a sort, and a very noble sort. Or, if we accept it because Jesus Himself, as we thus find and see Him, has utterly captured our moral will, our spiritual affections, our religious intuitions and imagination, and we are ready to follow Him to the world's end, then we become Christians of another, a more potent, perhaps a more distinctively religious, sort. As to His teaching and example, in which we are to put our trust if we follow Him, He Himself did not believe that all men could or would accept it. Many would be called and few chosen; the way was strait and narrow and few would there be who would go in thereat. But He certainly gave the assurance that all those who could and did accept His faith should overcome the world. Do we really believe that?

III. Now as to the teaching. Here we must be careful not to fall into the language of religious sentimentalism. The emotion of the gospel is a moral, an orderly emotion, an emotion which connotes ethical discipline. It is not romantic and uncritical, as it is so often presented. Let us begin with Jesus' teaching as to the nature and character of God. We find Him in that teaching rejecting the analogy of the physical world of power; doubtless unconscious of the analogy of metaphysical speculation; and using the familiar terms of the family relationships as the vehicles of His thought. One best senses what the character of the Infinite is like by symbolizing it under the human term of Father. No doubt other ethnic faiths have spoken of God as Father, but their Father-God has been a progenitor of a nation or a tribe and their brotherhood limited to racial lines. That is, they move on physical bases. Moreover, as these nations have progressed in culture the term Sovereign or Emperor has been substituted for Father. But in Christianity we find a reverse development; Jesus comes at the end of a long historical process and uses the word Father constantly as it has never been used in any other religion. His is the only developed religion which uses Father as the sign, the constant appellation of Deity. The ethical, and hence universal, Fatherhood dimly shadowed forth by Amos and Hosea, He teaches; a God who sendeth His rain on the just and on the unjust, and causes His sun to shine on the evil and on the good; a God who has an infinite care for men as His moral "children" so that the very hairs of their heads are all numbered. In this attributing to Deity the capacity and the will for infinite moral differentiation in His creatures is one of the most startling and original portions of the teaching of Jesus. No man, then, need ever be morally weak, for the Father desires to perfect that weakness in His strength. No man ever need be consumed with inward restlessness and discontent, for the Father waits to endow him with the abundance of His peace. No man need ever be morally shot to pieces and lost, because the Shepherd is always seeking His wandering sheep. No man need ever be discouraged by reason of the sins of his youth, for this is the Father who sees the prodigal coming a long way off and runs and falls on his neck and kisses him. But the gospel recognizes that many men will be weak; many are consumed with restlessness; many are lost; but there is no ultimate reason, outside of the mystery of the will of man, according to Jesus, why this should be so.

What then is the moral characteristic of the Father whom Jesus teaches? It is redemptive love, freely and supremely given, so that in the words of Jesus to the woman at the well, we know that God seeketh His true worshipers. It is redemptive love supremely exemplified in good will toward men, so that we see in the example of Jesus that He who knows that He comes from God and goes to God will, in His supreme moment of Godlikeness, gird Himself with a towel and wash His disciples' feet. We perceive then the social and disciplinary nature of the love of God as Jesus reveals it. It is a love whose purpose is character, whose content is service, whose method is glad devotion, whose goal is racial redemption. It is not a lazy, indulgent fondness; it is not a romantic or sentimental emotion; but it is a single-minded, educative, reformative, constructive love. The second element in the faith in Jesus is to accept this as man's best understanding of the nature of Deity.

Now this teaching is even more potently set forth in the conduct of Jesus than in His sayings. What He says is the character of God was His own character. Hence it follows, not as a matter of mystic vision, nor as a matter of philosophical speculation, but as a matter of experience, that the Christian conceives of the character of God in the terms of the character of Jesus, and when he is thinking of this aspect of divine life he says, in this realm, "God is like Jesus." The dreadful mistake which the historic Church has made has been to reverse that statement and thereby to render unintelligible the process, and to say "Jesus is like God," thus taking some preconceived conception of Deity, almost invariably conceived in terms of an absolute philosophy, and trying to read that into the Lord Jesus. Any notion, of whatever sort, which endeavors to identify Jesus with God, is religiously impious, intellectually indefensible, and ethically abhorrent. It would have been abhorrent to no one more than to Jesus Himself. But back of the great Christologies does lie a truth which I should say was the third fundamental of Christianity; namely, that the world has one adequate and satisfying conception as to the moral nature of Deity, so far as mankind needs or is able to understand it, and that conception is summed up in the person of Jesus. We find and worship God, through Jesus. Do we believe it?

IV. What then is, or should be, the universal belief as to what it means to be a disciple? It means to be a son and a brother in this kingdom, this divine family which Jesus preaches. And to be a son and a brother means to love our fellow men the way God loves us. That is to say, the attitude of the disciples of Jesus toward the human world is a loving, self-forgetful attitude, whose purpose is the making of Christian character, whose content is service, whose method is sacrifice, —if you mean by sacrifice glad and spontaneous devotion of all you have to the common good,—and whose goal is racial redemption. Thus we too serve men according to their need, not according to their desert. Thus we bless them that curse us, because an evil and a cursing heart needs blessing. Thus we pour out for men, and around them, an unexpected and undeserved affection, giving to the worst of them more than the best of them could ever have dreamed of, because the Father is more willing to hear than we to pray and has given us exceeding abundantly above all we could ask or think. Thus, to use the illustration of Jesus, when a man asks my coat I give him my cloak also, that he may know how my life reaches out toward him and that the only thing which limits my glad forth-giving to my neighbor is the extent of my perception of his need or the extent of his capacity to receive. The power comes when men live this way. Do we believe it?

The fundamental beliefs of Christianity, then, are: Faith in the moral and religious supremacy of Jesus, in the terms of active loyalty of the will to His principles, and standards of conduct, which loyalty finds its final sanction in the further faith, achieved through Him, that these principles and standards are of the essence of the Eternal Being and that their exemplification in motive and conduct is the most acceptable worship which mankind may offer Him. What doth the Lord require of us but to do justly and to love mercy and thus to walk humbly with our God?

Finally: The Christian power took its rise in a semimilitary, semicommercial imperialism with its characteristic accompaniments of the chattel slavery of the greater portion of its inhabitants and the moral and intellectual disintegration of its privileged classes. The Christian power, no longer advantaged by its pristine freshness and simplicity but, rather, encumbered by ancient institutionalized forms and inherited philosophies, faces to-day, as it has for the most part, throughout its history, a similar situation.

For, at this moment, the average man is beginning to discern that, behind the determining, as distinguished from the apparent, forces of this civilization, there lies a commercial and financial imperialism, directed by small but powerful minorities, largely supported by a sympathetic press, which uses the machinery of democracy to serve its own ends. The years between 1914 and 1923 have revealed the common springs of action of the professional soldier, politician, banker, captain of industry, ecclesiastic, in our present civilization. Allowing for numerous and occasionally notable exceptions, they accept, on the whole, the rule of force as the ultimate justification of conduct, with its accompanying materialism of faith and thought. And this rule of force has again the characteristic accompaniment of the industrial bondage of large masses of the population, and the decay of political vision and moral energy in its governing classes.

Yet the Christian spirit has persisted hitherto and the Christian power is not dead. In these two thousand years it has always mitigated, sometimes elevated and subdued, that imperialism and, from time to time, it has blossomed in luminous and self-verifying lives like Francis Xavier, Francis of Assisi, Father Damien, Wilfred Grenfell. It has always been to the worldly-wise foolishness, and to the amiable materialist a stumbling-block. It has probably never been more needed than at this desperate moment in the history of Western civilization. That spirit of Jesus may perish from the earth. If it is to survive, as I, for one, have no slightest doubt that it will, it will be because it can still command the allegiance of youth, who possess both moral and intellectual integrity, in this and the coming generations.

THE RETURN TO THEOLOGY

BENJAMIN W. BACON

Professor of New Testament Criticism and Interpretation, Yale Divinity School. Author of "Introduction to the New Testament" and "Jesus and Paul."

CHAPTER VI

THE RETURN TO THEOLOGY

BENJAMIN W. BACON

ONE of Molière's most amusing characters, on learning the distinction between poetry and prose, exclaims with great satisfaction at his own unexpected proficiency, "Why, I have been talking prose all my life without knowing it." I dislike to suggest that there is anything prosaic about theology, but I imagine that there are many of us who have similar unsuspected resources of culture. We have been talking theology all our lives without knowing it. We merely put our ideas about religion into terms of logic and common sense, and there it was, theology in spite of us.

In spite of us, I say, for until very recently, at least, it had been the fashion to decry theology. Religion? Yes; men believed in religion. Or if not, they tolerated it on the ground that "Man is incurably religious" and you may as well put up with what you can't help. Some regarded this instinct for religion as a misfortune superior persons must make the best of in their less enlightened neighbors. Others looked upon it as lifting humanity a little above the brutes, because you can have morality among animals, vicious horses and kindly ones, friendly elephants and man-killers. But we have yet to hear of a religious horse or dog. Perhaps religion is a relic of barbarianism, perhaps it is a proof of the kingdom of heaven. Either way we do appear to be "incurably religious." From the first faint glimmerings of archaeology to the remotest horizon of that future which we try to read in the reflected light of the past, man was religious in the beginning, is now, and ever will be.

Thomas Carlyle called religion "the deepest thing in man." He did not mean by the term, he said, what a man may profess or can be induced to subscribe to in public, but what deep down in his heart he is convinced of, and in his life actually adjusts himself to. His religion appears in the answers he gives to his own inmost soul when he reflects upon "the mysterious universe in which he finds himself, and his own Duty and Destiny in it."

Duty and Destiny—these are great words. Possibly you could impress some notion of the meaning of the former on an intelligent brute. You cannot convey the dimmest notion of the meaning of the latter. Possibly there may be a man so brutish as to have no idea of either. If there is, let him speak for himself. To our generation, with all its recklessness, all its revolt from everything that has come down from the past, all its rebellion against the voice of tradition or authority, they probably are just as full of potential meaning as to any earlier one. When we of to-day reflect upon "Duty and Destiny" does it mean a vague sentiment expressed in the formula, "Be good and you'll be happy"? Or does it mean that we are laboring to reach convictions such as character is built on? The difference between religion and theology is that one can be "religious" (or at least imagine oneself "religious") on a vague sentiment, or a feeling of aesthetic aspiration, but one cannot be "theological" without logic.

It is fair to assume that all of us are "religious" to

at least the extent of having some interest in matters of Duty and Destiny. I think most of us will concede to Carlyle also, that the universe in which we happen to find ourselves has involved both these terms in no small element of "mystery." It has made thinking on the subject hard. Duty and Destiny are delicate subjects. With just the right person, in just the right circumstances, we have sometimes "talked religion." We were even glad of the chance. But theology? No! not unless like Molière's Bourgeois Gentilhomme we talked it without knowing it—as perhaps we did.

Theology is supposed to be remote from all the real and practical interests of life. There was a time, they say, when the fish-wives in the market-place of Alexandria disputed the great doctrines of the Church. Publishers will tell you there was a time when theological books were "the best sellers." To-day, to command a market, your theological book must either be provocative (that is, it must be "polemic" theology) or else it must have real merit, as the result of hard, logical thinking. But in the latter case it should not be labeled "theology." Yes, I know, thinking people are really keen for the kind of thing Professor Hocking can tell them in his *Meaning of God in Human Experience,* or Professor Mackintosh in his *Theology as an Empirical Science.* Only, if you are thinking of writing a treatise on theology take a leaf from the book of Mrs. Gamp, who when her sentences chanced to rhyme explained to Betsy Prig that if she was making poetry it was "not intentional."

It is pleasant to learn that so excellent a book as Professor Hocking's has gone through a series of printings. It shows that people will read worth-while books on this subject. But people who bought Hocking's book probably thought it was philosophy or psychology. Men and women really do crave to know the best of human thought on these mysterious subjects of Duty and Destiny. But when they are offered treatises on systematic theology, they decline. I wonder why.

It is more than manifest that men do wish to know about religion. It is pathetic. It recalls the great saying in Augustine's Confessions: "O God, thou hast created us for thyself, and our souls are restless till they find rest in Thee." Most of all since the War, which has made peace on earth and good will among men seem a thousand miles farther off than it was before we fought, there is a reaction toward religion that astonishes observers. If ever Christian civilization (so-called) proved its own disastrous failure it is now. And yet, in this near-collapse of Christendom, men seem to realize instinctively that the only trouble with Christianity was that there was so little of it. Labor men erect class-loyalty into a religion. Politicians try to base new popular movements on religious motives, wholesome or poisonous. Charlatans, healers, mind-curists, and sober-minded medical men have religious (or quasi-religious) cures, by which circumambient spirit can be made to act on the body. Evangelists and preachers, some ignorant, some educated, have moral cures, by which circumambient spirit can be made to act on the conscience and character. You hear of strange reactions in the churches, some superstitious, some enlightened, some pretending to be enlightened when only superstitious, some hopeful, some sinister, and with it all an immense addition to the rolls of Church-membership. A starving, agonizing, half-ruined earth looks up to heaven in the bitter consciousness that it carries within it the seeds of its own destruction, a remorseful, shamed, despairing humanity cries out to its Creator: Wherefore didst Thou make all men in vain? O wretched man that I am, who shall deliver me from the body of this death? Humanity instinctively turns to religion as the only possible way out. Oh, for the old sense of Duty. Oh, for the former hope of a happier Destiny! "Religion" is the cry; not "theology." Emotion, but not reason. Feeling, but not thinking. Impulse, but not logic or experience.

But that is not our method in business affairs. Business takes the road to ruin the moment we relax the control of strict, hard thinking and wise experience. How long can we afford to commit the interests of religion to uncontrolled emotion? Bishop Gore of Oxford and a group of Anglican writers address the world in a recent book called *The Return to Christendom.* The writers show a keen realization of the necessity of Christianizing the social order. Democracy, they believe, is fast yielding to plutocracy, or else to the mutually destructive struggle between plutocracy and the proletariat. Christendom is nearing collapse. What, then, is the remedy? Back to medievalism. A return to the Christendom of ecclesiastical control. Back to the vision of Augustine and Bernard, the Commonwealth of God, under the Vicar of St. Peter and the Church councils. Yes, they say, let us appeal to the instinct of religion, but keep it under control of "dogma," as defined by prelates and councils. Let the Church define orthodoxy and supply the public with what the bishop lays down. The public requires to be catechized and disciplined, and the heterodox to be silenced.

But the bishop himself declines to say what is orthodox. That is not the function of a bishop, whose office is executive rather than legislative. Once more the layman is thrown back upon "private judgment." So medievalism breaks down of its own weight. It refuses to assume the very responsibility it asked for.

Modernism has already won the field. Anglo-catholicism cannot save Christianity at the expense of democracy in England, any more than ignorant dictatorship can bind it in this country with the decrees of a Kentucky legislature. The domination of dogma is a hopeless dream, even if it were desirable. Religion will be an instinct of humanity ten thousand years hence as truly as to-day. But freedom of religious thinking has come to stay. There is to be a religion of the future, a Christianity of the future; but not under the domination of Pope or proletariat. It will not be religion without logic, emotion without thought, impulse without conviction; for we do not mean our children to be swept back into the wild fanaticism of ignorant and superstitious savages. Religion will be under the control of reason and conscience, educated, free, democratic. It will have theology, but not scholasticism; doctrine, but not dogma. It will have the ethics, conviction, and character of the open forum of scientific debate. The bishop declines to think for you. Thank heaven. Think for yourself.

It is this kind of theology to which Professor Francis Peabody welcomes our "Return" in a recent number of the *Yale Review*. Professor Peabody is a veteran exponent of Christianity, a scholar known and loved on both sides of the Atlantic, and a firm adherent of that branch of the Church which goes farthest in the direction of Christian liberty and enlightenment. Therefore, if Professor Peabody sees and welcomes a Return to Theology, I rejoice at the good news. Men are actually beginning to think that reason, logic, science, experience, criticism, have something to do with religious belief and conduct. It seems too good to be true. But with God all things are possible.

Down to Reformation times people believed that they maintained priests and prelates to save themselves the trouble of thinking in matters of religion. Real thinking is hard anyway, and religious thinking has special difficulties of its own, some natural, some artificial. For a thousand years after Christianity was established in the Empire the people called in the specialists, and the specialists asked acceptance of their results without inspection—*fides implicita.* The result was stagnation of thought for a thousand years, repression, explosion. After the Reformation came a new attempt along similar lines. It was less trouble for the laity, and much less for the clergy, if you could make a miraculous book take the place of thinking. So the post-Reformation dogmatists followed the example of the Rabbis, and told the laity the Bible was a substitute for thinking. Some people welcome the assurance that too much thinking is bad for the laity. But most Americans are democrats. In malice, let us hope, they are babies; but in understanding they aspire to be full-grown men. They dislike having the decisions made for them. Quite a lot of them are Baptists, and believe in democracy in the Church, freedom of religious opinion, and religious education. Therefore when Professor Peabody heard the echoes from Indiana in the summer of 1922, he sat down like an old prophet and wrote that article full of hope called "A Return to Theology." Is it true?

Unfortunately ready-made theology is cheap and easy, and the self-made is hard. So it must be until somebody discovers the royal road to learning. Meantime you will be plagued to death by people who want to take the job of religious thinking for you at the cheapest rates. They will charge you nothing for it because it costs them nothing. You can have a million copies for a few cents. But it is very expensive at the price. It costs personal effort to do your own thinking. It costs more in the realm of religion than anywhere else. But it is worth while. Popes and priests, and politicians and popular preachers will be only too delighted to make up your mind for you, if you will let them. Then you will give them your votes and influence. But that is the weakness of democracy; it's such an unending lot of trouble. You have to keep everlastingly at it, thinking, and thinking, and thinking. And the moment you let up, along comes some charlatan and induces you to part with your birthright for a mess of pottage. Eternal vigilance is the price of liberty.

But there is another, more special, reason for a return to theology. Ministers too—some of them—were dodging the hard kind of thinking. Even some of the so-called systematic theologians were doing it. The recent incumbent of one of the most illustrious chairs in America told me some years ago that he could only accept the appointment on the understanding that his courses were really to be in the history of doctrine. That is, he was going to make himself a mere echo of the past. That is safer and easier, of course, than saying: This is the problem; here is the evidence; what is the logical conclusion? Perhaps echoing the past is all we have a right to expect from our systematic theologians; unfortunately in a good many cases it is all we are getting. And when I realized how much alleged systematic theology consists of what somebody else thought on the great problems of life, somewhere from three hundred to two thousand years ago, I cease to wonder so much that people don't care to buy it. The fact is, I am not particularly anxious myself to read what Edwards, or Calvin, or Anselm, thought about the Trinity, or life after death.

But what about the doctrinal sermons? Are the preachers leading their people to think on the great religious problems? Last week a gentleman spoke to me of a great sermon he had just heard. "I was afraid," said he, "it was going to be doctrinal." But to his great relief it turned out to be a practical exhortation. For a full generation now we have heard "ethical preaching." We have been told which way to turn, but nothing as to where we are going. Right conduct has been the end in view, what ought to be done by the individual, the Church, the nation, the state, the schools, the family, society, the shop, the newspaper; ethics of home, of state, of business, of politics, of economics, of international relations, of every other kind of relations. There has been no end of it. And there ought to be none. After so many generations of a kind of Christianity whose main business seemed to be the getting one's own miserable soul out of the punishment it deserved, it was time to forget that I have

A never dying soul to save
And fit it for the sky.

It was time to remember that the Author of this salvation went about saying "He that would save his soul shall lose it, and whosoever will lose his soul for my sake and the gospel's, the same shall save it." Yes, surely it was worth while to have at least one generation of "ethical preaching," to cry out, Duty, Duty, Duty, in a world that cannot be saved without the intervention of God. It was worth while to have one generation learn what Jesus meant when He came proclaiming: "The kingdom of God is at hand. Seek that first. Live for it. Die for it."

But it is also worth while to give a little thought to what you mean by this word "God," and this phrase "the kingdom of God." It is worth while also to have some notion of Destiny, as well as Duty. Unless men have spirits as well as bodies, never-dying souls appointed for some kind of Destiny, working for the kingdom of God seems to me to stand on about the same level as working for public sanitation, or hygienics, or eugenics, or an Antipoverty League. John Smith calls to you as you pass: "Hey, there. I hear you are a minister of the gospel. Tell us about it." So you tell him of your economics, eugenics, and hygienics. "Is that all?" says John Smith. "All this have I heard from my youth. Let us continue to eat and drink, for to-morrow we die." How many uplifters we have, whose gospel is, "Improve the conditions, and man's spirit will improve itself." When I was a boy humanity had become master of the world in one dimension. Steam transportation by land and sea, and steam manufacture, had opened enormous natural resources. Recently we have added two dimensions more. We now control the depths of the sea and the upper air. The first use of the new power was enormous devastation, the submarine and the bombing airplane. By high explosives and poison gas it is now possible to destroy in a few months all the accumulations of a thousand years of civilization. Note the vast improvement of the human spirit through scientific, mechanical, and economic progress.

Or perhaps we should pin our hopes to social and political progress. There is the splendid example of Russia, and the sovietizing of industry in the rest of the world. Jesus undoubtedly desired a new and better social order. But Jesus was not a socialist, and pulpit and soapbox do not stand for the same thing. We have apostles of good health who would make the Church a clinic, or a gymnasium. Jesus healed. But He did not come to be a healer. He avoided the importunities of the sick in body that He might have opportunity to minister to the sick in soul. I myself like healthy men. But I have seen some saints who were not, and were of more use to the world than their healthy neighbors. Christians must seek first the kingdom of God. And a right spirit in individuals and the body politic is quite as important for the kingdom of God as healthy bodies, though healthy bodies are desirable also.

Where are we going? What are we aiming at? What do we mean when we talk of "consecration to the ideals of Jesus Christ"? These are practical questions, however "theological." They are fundamental questions of the urgent inexorable present, questions of Duty and Destiny in the mysterious universe in which we find ourselves. Poor and rich, sick and well, we have to meet them with an answer. Whether economic conditions are improved or not, whether health and sanitation are improved or not, whether we live or die, these questions will not wait. We must do our living for to-day and to-morrow by the answers we frame for them. What is our Duty? What is our Destiny?

It might, then, be well for ministers who have the leisure to teach a little theology. They should not advertise a class in the subject unless prepared to find an attendance of half the number expected, but they might try once in a while to give a rationally thought-out reply to the questions men have to answer for themselves without knowing that this is theology: "Who, or what, is God"? "What does He expect of me?" "What may I expect of Him?" The questions may be asked and answered perfunctorily, catechism-fashion; or they may be answered in words that have been

> fierily furnaced
> In the blast of a soul that has struggled in earnest.

If answered in the latter way they will not lack interest. But the answers will not be easy.

There is still another reason why men in our generation are seeking fresh answers to these age-long questions. The War waked us up to a realizing sense that they do not stay answered from one generation to the next. If you think that a past theology can serve the present age, then you should read the reports of some of our army chaplains, and see what pitiful, perfunctory, unreal stuff our young men believed to be Christianity, or else believed they ought to believe as Christianity.

> We had forgotten You, or very nearly—
> You did not seem to touch us very nearly—
> Of course we thought about You now and then;

Especially in any time of trouble—
We knew that You were good in time of trouble—
  But we are very ordinary men.

* * * * *

Now we remember, over here in Flanders—
(It isn't strange to think of You in Flanders)—
  This hideous warfare seems to make things clear.
We never thought about You much in England—
But now that we are far away from England—
  We have no doubts, we know that You are here.

We think about You kneeling in the garden—
Ah, God, the agony of that dread garden—
  We know You prayed for us upon the cross.
If anything could make us glad to bear it
'Twould be the knowledge that You willed to bear it—
  Pain, death, the uttermost of human loss.

Though we forgot You—You will not forget us—
We feel so sure that You will not forget us—
  But stay with us until this dream is past.
And so we ask for courage, strength, and pardon—
Especially, I think, we ask for pardon—
  And that You'll stand beside us to the last.

That is the pathetic cry of a perfunctory and conventional Christian teaching, suddenly awakened to the realization that the "word of the cross" is all the gospel, all the religion that we have; and that we now must make the most of it, though we had "never thought about You much in England." Does our Christianity mean much to us, or does it mean nothing but a dream?

Some time ago I had an answer to a question on the Epistle to the Hebrews in an examination paper. The student told me that its unknown author "rambled through the whole field of theology." That was a sincere and a revealing word. It meant that nothing in that splendid oration of Hebrews had "touched that student very nearly." To him it was mere religious words out of a past that was alien and unreal to him. Hebrews is a writing by an unknown Christian leader of the second generation, who is sending a message to his regiment, a few moments before the zero hour, when they have got to go "over the top." He himself cannot be with them. He is an exile or a prisoner; but he calls to mind the martyrdom of the Captain and Pioneer of their salvation, Jesus, who fulfilled it before Pontius Pilate but a few short years before. It is a thrilling call to heroism, ringing with the courage and faith of one himself prepared to tread in the footsteps of the great High Priest of humanity, who now stands in the presence of God.

But of course we read our Bibles to-day as did the eunuch of Candace, of whom Philip asked, "Understandest thou what thou readest?" Men have to answer to-day as the eunuch did, "How can I, except some man guide me?" Well, a twentieth-century American could not be expected to enter into the spirit of a first-century Alexandrian, and realize what he was reading, unless some man would guide him. So I do not wonder that my student thought the author of Hebrews was just "rambling through the whole field of theology." In reality this unknown officer in the Church of the generation after Paul was showing to his followers how the whole system of sacrifice and ritual, priesthood, temple, festivals, and sacrifice instituted in the past, had given way now to a new reality. We have access now, "by a new and living way," to the God that before could only be reached through temples and ritual observances. Jesus the martyr, Jesus the true and eternal Priest, has entered before us into the very presence of His Father, the 'Father' of Jesus' prayers. That is the Being whom again and again this writer calls "the living God," the God of actuality, not of the book-religion of the past. Jesus, to him, brought God near.

That is what the martyrdom of the great High Priest of humanity did for his brethren two thousand years ago. Jesus "brought men near" to His Father as "the living God." It is pathetic that men should be still crying out to-day for guidance to the God and Father of our Lord Jesus Christ, as the living God. That was the God who really does things, the God whom Jesus trusted, the God that seemed to forsake Him on the cross, and then made Him the Author of an eternal salvation, the God not of the past, nor of a book, but the God of things as they really are. Do we, to-day, really guide men to the living God? Isaiah said to the men of his time:

> All vision is become to you as the words of a book that is sealed, which men deliver to one that is learned, saying, Read this, I pray thee; and he saith, I cannot, for it is sealed. (If I tell you what is really there I shall be stoned and silenced and cast out of the Church.) And the book is delivered to him that is not learned, saying, Read this, I pray thee; and he saith, I am not learned.

Nobody knows the name of the author of Hebrews. He had heard something, probably not a great deal, from eyewitnesses and ministers of the word in the generation before, of the martyrdom of Jesus. He knew of Jesus' prayer and suffering to bring humanity back into right relation with God. He knew the story of His kneeling in the garden—"Ah, God, the agony of that dread garden"—and he thought that story of the cross worth more to religion than all the ritual of temple and shrine, sacrifice and offering of bulls and goats from Melchizedek down. He had found in this brother man, obedient unto the death of the cross, a real and living Priest, a Mediator, who had passed into the presence of the living God, and who ever liveth there, to make intercession for us.

I admit that this unknown author is a theologian. He has read the great works of Plato and Philo, and can handle the splendors of Greek rhetoric with greater ease than any other writer of the New Testament. But this is not his title to greatness. His greatness lies in his realizing sense, similar to that of Paul, that the living God had spoken in his time, that the story of what Jesus did is a revelation, a restoration of lost humanity by the intervention of One who through this Great Shepherd of the sheep brought us into the new and eternal covenant of peace. In the spirit of Jesus he had suddenly caught a vision of God, the real, the actual, the "living God."

What, then, was this story which this unknown writer knew, eclipsing all the revelations of former times? Is it to us also a revelation of the living God? This cultured Alexandrian knew that Jesus, a Galilean carpenter of the generation just before his own, had come forward after the martyrdom of John, the Elijah of that generation, taking up John's work and carrying it to its completion. Jesus himself looked on John as sent by God to accomplish the Great Repentance, turning the heart of Israel back again, as Elijah did at Carmel, so that the day of Jehovah's coming might not smite the earth with a curse. A Jewish writer two hundred years before had declared this task of Elijah to be the reconciliation of Jehovah to his sinful people.

Elijah, he says, was recorded for reproofs in their seasons,
To pacify anger before it brake forth into wrath;
To turn the heart of the Father (God) unto the son (Israel)
And to restore the tribes of Jacob.

Jesus conceived the work of John as that "restoration of all things" in a great repentance of Israel which should bring about reconciliation to "the Father" ere it should be too late. There is the background of the story of Jesus. When John was shut up in prison Jesus came forward and took up the prophet's message. He carried it on in Galilee, and Peraea and Jerusalem, predicting that he would be made to share the fate of John. He did. He also suffered the same things of them, in the city that slew the prophets, and stoned them that were sent unto her. So much we may be sure the author of Hebrews knew of the earthly life of Jesus; for so much is implied in the great letters of Paul, some of which this writer uses. Jesus came, as Paul says, "preaching peace to him that is far off, and peace to him that is nigh, because both Jew and Gentile, near and far off, have access in one Spirit—His Spirit—unto the Father." It was a work of reconciliation of Father to son, and son to Father, in repentance and forgiveness. Jesus meant it for His own people. He felt called to serve them first. Paul extended the reconciliation idea to all estranged humanity.

What the author of Hebrews had was a mere story, a bit of recent martyrology. Jesus, to accomplish the religious ideal of His nation, had done what Quintus Curtius and other heroes did to accomplish the military ideals of their nations. What makes Jesus' story more than a hero-tale? What makes it a "gospel," a revelation of God? What gives it eternal significance to people that want to know who God is, what He expects of them, what they may expect of Him? What made the story of Calvary an "eternal" gospel? The part of God in it. Well, what did God do? According to these ancient writers He made Jesus the agent by which humanity in its wickedness and misery was brought back to Himself. "The very God of peace," says this writer, "brought again from the dead our Lord Jesus, that great Shepherd of the sheep, through the blood of an eternal covenant,"—the "new covenant" of forgiveness, laws written on the heart, filial relations with a Father-God—so that this living God might "make us all perfect, working in us, through the spirit of Jesus, what is well pleasing to himself."

The author of Hebrews believes God does that through Jesus, for individuals—for the world. Well, does He? Try it. Let the world try it. That is the only way to know whether it is so or not. Try it, and put down your results. That will be empirical theology: what God did, what God does. Does He, did He, restore not only Israel, but a whole groaning, perishing world to His favor and peace through the spirit of Jesus? That is the practical question.

Go back a step from the author of Hebrews to Paul, the man who took the story of Jesus' work for the reconciliation of Israel, and made it applicable to humanity.

This is the apostolic message in the very words of the first theologian of the Church:

All things are of God, who reconciled (mankind) to himself through Christ, and gave unto us (heralds of the cross) the ministry of the Reconciliation; to wit, that God through the agency of Christ was restoring the world to his favor, not reckoning unto men their trespasses. And he hath committed unto us the message of the Reconciliation. We (apostles) therefore are ambassadors on behalf of Christ, as though God were entreating by us; we beseech you on behalf of Christ, accept this restoration to God's favor.

I know that Paul must have told the story of the cross as part of his message, because he alludes to the fact as characterizing his preaching at Corinth. I know he must have related the incidents of the farewell supper; because in correcting abuses in the celebrations at Corinth he reminds them of the story of "the same night in which he was betrayed," and bids them remember that in the ritual "ye are telling the story (*καταγγέλλετε*) of the Lord's death until he come." But I am not so foolish as to imagine that Paul thought he could offer the world a "gospel of peace" by anything which does not bring men into contact with the living God by showing Him at work. Telling men the beautiful system of ethics Jesus taught in Galilee does not give them a gospel. Telling the marvels of healing that took place while He went about preaching repentance is not a gospel. Telling how He was martyred for the kingdom's sake is not a gospel, unless somehow, somewhere, you can show that the hand of the living eternal God was at work in the matter.

Now that is just the part that historical criticism

leaves out. Not because it questions it, or doubts it, or objects to it; but simply because criticism is historical and not theological. It undertakes to say what happened. "Did God have anything to do with its happening that way?" you ask. "I don't know," says criticism. "I am not a theologian. That is none of my business."

But Paul *was* a theologian. Knowing from his letters what he thought of his commission from God I am not surprised to find that Paul never mentions a single mighty work of Jesus, and scarcely ever a saying. He knew that you cannot save a lost world by anything which does not bring them into contact with the God and Father of our Lord Jesus Christ. If by the story of the cross you can give men a solution of their problems of Duty and Destiny then you have a gospel. Did this Galilean know this living God and solve our bitter problem? If so He has something to say to us. If not, He is just one more Teacher of another system of ethics, a little better than some of the others that went before. If Jesus knew God, and how to live and die in the peace of God, and how to bring men near to God, then He is worthy to be called the world's Christ—not merely Israel's Christ, but the Christ of humanity. For that is what humanity needs. It needs to be "shown the Father." If Jesus can do that, if He can give us His peace, He has a gospel for us. Paul, the theologian apostle, thinks that Jesus does give men through the spirit in which He lived and died—if we can define it—"access to the Father." Paul's follower thinks that Jesus shows a "new and living way" by which men can come to the Father. He thinks the very God of peace made Him the author of "an eternal salvation" for all humanity. At all events, this layman of Nazareth does make religion something real, not the mere dead letter of a book.

Paul is the first Christian theologian. After Calvary the eleven sat down and drew lots as to who should fill the place of Judas. They made up their minds as to what the world really needed.

> Of the men, therefore, that have companied with us all the time that the Lord Jesus went in and went out among us, beginning from the baptism of John, unto the day that he was received up from us, of these must one become a witness with us of his resurrection.

Such were the qualifications of an Apostle as the eleven conceived it. Such is the testimony we try to get from criticism. They thought the world needed to be told the anecdotes and the sayings that they could remember, and testify before courts to the reality of the resurrection body as having seen it themselves. There you have all the marks of an apostleship through men, by a man. So they drew lots, as between Joseph and Matthias, and decided that because it did not fall on Joseph, therefore the Lord (!) had chosen Matthias. So he was numbered with the eleven apostles, and that is the last that was ever heard of him.

And the Lord Himself set to work to choose His own apostle, not from men, neither through a man, but by appointment direct from heaven. And He chose Saul of Tarsus, a man that had never seen Jesus in the flesh, and if he had, tells us in so many words that he would "forget it." The eleven chose Matthias. Doubtless he could tell ever so many anecdotes about Jesus' doings and sayings, about how He looked and acted; for had he not companied with the apostles the whole time from the baptism of John to the Ascension? And God chose Paul, and made him the herald of a world gospel "from Jerusalem round about unto Illyricum," the second founder of the faith, who made it a message of redemption for the whole world, simply because he realized that God was restoring the world in Christ.

Thank the Lord that He chose one theologian! Thank God for one apostle who knew himself to be charged by the Lord with a message to all humanity! Thank God for one man who could see the real significance of the events that had taken place, either because (or in spite of) the fact that he had originally set out to persecute this Way unto the death! For Saul of Tarsus knew that as between Pharisaism, the religion of the Book, and this new Way of access to the living God and Father of our Lord Jesus Christ, there must be war to extermination. There is no truce between Law and Gospel. Either you can be saved by obeying the precepts of a book, according to the application of a lot of learned interpreters who sit in Moses' seat, or else you cannot. Paul had tried Pharisaism to the bitter end, and knew that you cannot have peace with God that way. That way "a wrath of God is manifested," as it is written, "cursed is every one that abideth not in all things that are written in the book of the law to do them." The law cannot give life, because of the inherent weakness of human flesh. It is an ordinance of death, a sentence, a judgment, a condemnation. Then, if you cannot escape the wrath of the God of righteousness by any attempted obedience to moral precepts, is there any escape? The Christians said there was. They believed in forgiveness through the grace of the Lord Jesus. They believed that He had gone into the presence of God, there to make intercession for their forgiveness. Whether He had or not, they knew God was "in him." They had seen "the living God" in His face. That was religion, gospel. It brought them "near" to God.

Of course, Paul, a scribe and Pharisee, who believed in a divine revelation to Moses, and that the one hope of redemption for the world lay in submission to this holy law, would have to be a persecutor to the death of such a doctrine as the gospel of Jesus. It gave an entirely new way of reconciliation with God, utterly inconsistent with the law and the prophets. Tolerate it, and you threw open the doors of the kingdom of heaven to every miserable believer, worthy or unworthy. You took away the prerogative of Israel. You offered a new Way of acceptance, reconciliation, peace with God, to Tom, Dick, and Harry, Jew or Greek, barbarian, Scythian, bondman, freeman. Can you imagine a Pharisee of Pharisees, a Hebrew of Hebrews, of the tribe of Benjamin, a zealot for the law, tolerating that kind of doctrine? Not while he believed in Moses, and a righteousness of his own, even that which is through the law. That was Saul, the Pharisee.

But Jesus Christ needed a theologian to take the real meaning of His work and make it clear to humanity. God needed a theologian to teach men that the gospel is the thing that He does and will do through the agency of this eternal Christ of mankind, not a lot of anecdotes about the sayings and doings of Jesus, and how He was seen in vision after He had risen from the dead, by men that had companied with Him. God needed an ambassador of peace to the world. God needed a man who realized what humanity needs as Paul realized it. God needed a messenger to tell how a man can have peace with the real and living God, the God and Father of our Lord Jesus Christ. And so while the eleven were drawing lots to see whether Joseph or Matthias would make the best successor to Judas Iscariot, God chose Paul. He needed such a man to be a minister of a new Covenant—not that old Covenant of Sinai, which since Jeremiah's time scribes had been vainly trying to impose on men as a kind of book religion, but a new covenant of the forgiveness of sins, as it is written:

> Behold, the days come, saith the Lord, that I will make a new covenant with the house of Israel and with the house of Judah. . . . For this is the covenant that I will make with the house of Israel after those days, saith the Lord; I will put my laws into their mind, and on their heart also will I write them. And I will be to them a God, and they shall be to me a people. . . . For I will be merciful to their iniquities, and their sins will I remember no more.

Paul, and the writer of Hebrews, knew what Jeremiah meant by his prophecy of the "new covenant" of the living God with His redeemed people. Paul realized that the story of the cross, as something that God had done "through the agency of Christ," was a gospel of peace from God, to a world lying in darkness and condemnation. He probably knew very little of the life of Jesus. He knew about what he could learn in a two weeks' visit at Jerusalem from James the Lord's brother, and the Apostle Peter. He knew what sort of character it produces, when a man's whole heart and soul and strength and mind are consecrated to one thing only, the doing of the will of his Father, and the sanctifying of His name on earth. Paul could know what sort of spirit the spirit of Jesus was, and how it corresponded with that spirit of the Servant of Jehovah of whom Isaiah had written. Therefore he could urge men who wanted like unity with God to "have in them the mind which was in Christ Jesus," who "humbled himself and took upon him the form of a Servant, and became obedient unto death, even the death of the cross." That was enough.

Paul probably had never heard the story of the virgin birth. If he had ever heard of any of the miracles he gives no sign of it. He says that Jesus "knew no sin," but he did not learn even that by enquiries at Nazareth as to whether Jesus obeyed His mother when He was a little boy. He found it written in the prophecy of Isaiah of the suffering Servant. Paul simply knew that by this man's devotion of Himself to death for the sake of God's kingdom, the people that had been estranged from God were reconciled. God had made the Carpenter of Nazareth His agent to accomplish the reconciliation.

What then, did it matter to this Apostle of the Gentiles whether this man that God had chosen to lift the ban from humanity was the wisest that ever lived, or the simplest, whether He had the power of God, or was "crucified through weakness," though living now through the power of God; whether He was an archangel or just a Galilean Teacher and Leader of the publicans and sinners to repentance? What does it matter to us whether this theologian Paul, like some later ones, was led off into metaphysics in his endeavor to identify that eternal redeeming spirit of God that was in Christ, starting speculation along the dubious lines of the Logos doctrine? We can make our own metaphysics. We can make our own Logos doctrine. What does it matter to us, who have our own theology to make, and who desire only to see God in Christ, how Paul adjusted his beliefs concerning the preëxistent Wisdom of God, creative and redemptive, to his thought of Christ, so long as we know from the testimony that God was "in him"? His work was God's work. To us also the glory of the redeeming, forgiving God is revealed in the face of Jesus Christ. We have faith in this God, because He is the God and Father of our Lord Jesus Christ.

Beside this manifestation of God "in the face of Jesus Christ," as visible to us to-day as it was to Paul, it does not matter whether the virgin birth story, and the miracles of walking on the sea, raising of the dead, or changing water to wine, are fact or legend, history or wonder-story. Did God make of Jesus His agent to restore the world to His favor, not imputing unto men their trespasses? Had the eternal, the "living" God, done this; and is He doing it now? If so, that is "the eternal gospel." And that you can verify for yourself, as Paul verified it. That the world can verify if it will. This, I say, is our modern return to theology. We are brought through this man Jesus to know His Father in heaven, Jew and Gentile, barbarian, Scythian, bondman, freeman, near and far-off, we are brought nigh in one spirit—His spirit—unto the common Father. That may be theology, but it is also fact. It is an eternally self-verifiable truth, whenever individuals, or the world, are willing to put it to the test. Get all the facts you can from Matthias, from criticism, and then go to the theologian Paul, and ask: Had God anything to do with this, or not?

Can a man, through the spirit of Jesus have access to God? Can he have a religion which solves for him the problem of Duty and Destiny? That is a question first of all of experience, afterwards of "theology." Paul had both. For a generation or so Christian pulpits have been resounding with ethics. Our ministers have all been Matthiases. We have been incessantly bombarded with new discoveries or supposed discoveries about the career and teaching of Jesus. Criticism has been called upon to tell the last atom of truth, or supposed truth, that could be wrung from the scanty records to tell what Jesus said and did, what He looked like, where He ate and slept and walked. Read all your critical and pseudo-critical and fanciful and historical and every other kind of lives of Christ. It *is* of great importance. I myself have devoted a lifetime to it. I am not going to disparage its value. If there was no historical Jesus we simply do not know what we are talking about when we say God made this humble Nazarene His agent for the redemption of humanity. But after you have done all that thank God for one theologian apostle, that had the insight to realize that what the world needs is to have access to God, and that through the spirit of Jesus a man can have it.

Is there, or is there not, in our time, the beginning of a return to theology? By the grace of God I believe there is. I believe men really are beginning to want to know something about the living God. The God that is actually at work around us and in us, the very same of whom Paul said, quoting a heathen poet, "For in him we live and move and have our being." Really men are coming to think it is worth while to think about Duty and Destiny in this mysterious universe in which we find ourselves, and that it does even matter to us what the purest, noblest, most God-loving, devoted man that ever lived felt toward this God that seemed to have forsaken Him on the cross.

We think about You kneeling in the garden—
Ah, God, the agony of that dread garden—
  We know You prayed for us upon the cross.
If anything could make us glad to bear it—
'Twould be the knowledge that You willed to bear it—
  Pain, death, the uttermost of human loss.

Though we forgot You—You will not forget us—
We feel so sure that You will not forget us—
  But stay with us until this dream is past.
And so we ask for courage, strength, and pardon—
Especially I think, we ask for pardon—
  And that You'll stand beside us to the last.

LIFE AFTER DEATH

WILLARD L. SPERRY

Dean of the Theological School in Harvard University.
Author of "The Discipline of Liberty."

CHAPTER VII

LIFE AFTER DEATH

WILLARD L. SPERRY

WHEN Henry Thoreau lay dying in Concord his brother came to him seeking some expression of confidence in the life hereafter. Thoreau, running perfectly true to form, looked up and with a wan smile said, "One world at a time, brother, one world at a time."

This wholesome gospel of one world at a time represents the major mood of our modern practical Christianity. To live rightly and well in this world is our plain duty and the best possible preparation for any world hereafter. There is among us, or at least there was before the War, a disinclination to linger too long in the presence of the fact of death, a tendency to dismiss it sentimentally rather than to grapple with it and wrest from it some kind of answer to the problem it presents. The War, however, has altered that mood. A fresh and fearless realism has come into our thinking. Death has become an accepted and inevitable fact of common life. "In every cottage in England," said an Oxford don, "there is to-day a monument to unanswered prayer." What was in quieter days the occasional sombre event in the community became the norm. Our generation, with its ten millions of men untimely dead in War, no longer shirks the fact and the problem, and is no longer indifferent to the further hope. All over the world the old question is asked with new insistency, "If a man die shall he live again?"

May I deal first with the attempts to give a scientific answer to this question? Science has to do with the world of immediate sense experience. It aims to order and to interpret that world. The great religious systems of the past and of the present have assumed that we do not have and cannot have sense experience of any other life in any other world than this, and that therefore the assurance of immortality belongs to those realms discovered by supernatural revelation or essayed by acts of faith.

The latest and most ambitious of the sciences is the would-be science of psychical research. It has yet to make good its place as a science of the first rank. But the boldness of its assertions and the comfort which it has undoubtedly offered to thousands of perplexed and sorrowful persons in the modern world entitle it to serious attention. In the immediate past, as in the present, it has had the sanction and support of many of the finer and more adventurous spirits in the world of philosophy and theology. And no scientist of the first rank is prepared to deny all validity to its proceedings.

The sole aim of this science is to vindicate the continuance of conscious personality after death, with the memory, the affections, the purposes, which make up personal life. We should not dismiss the "messages" received because they seem to be trivial. It is by trivial bits of evidence that the truthfulness of the witness is confirmed. This science has no immediate interest to discover and announce what heaven is like, since there is no way of "checking up" evidence upon that matter. But it is jealous for those stray intimations, coming from the unknown world, as to what happened in this world, because such evidence can be proved or disproved here below. For that reason the Society for Psychical Research is far more soberly concerned with what they conceive Professor James has said about his "pink pyjamas," than in his account of the hereafter. The "pink pyjamas" and all for which they stand can be verified; heaven cannot be verified by any checking system available to us. Religiously we deplore the references to such trivial and mundane paraphernalia, but scientifically we must be jealous for them. The society in question has gathered, through its sittings and mediums, a body of alleged communications as to facts in the lives of persons now dead which is very challenging. It is difficult to understand, in many cases, how knowledge of these facts could be present in the mind, conscious or subconscious, of the medium or in the mind of any sitter. Science is always bound to accept the simpler and more immediate solution as against the more involved and remote solution. At times it is hard to resist the conclusion that this science-in-the-making does prove its case. I can only confess in my own case and plead in the case of others that open-mindedness which is the welcome waiting for each new discovery in the world.

There is, however, one serious ethical consideration in the case which seems to me to deserve mention. I have it upon the word of a man who gave the latter part of his life almost entirely to this concern, that the medium through whom the messages are received must be a person of unstable mental stuff. There must be some "crack" or flaw in the earthen vessel. The medium is not a normal person. Moreover, the state of trance is a great mental strain upon the medium, tending toward greater mental instability. So much is this so that no reputable enquirer makes undue demand upon his medium. One seance or two a week are all that can be sanctioned. Beyond that lies undue strain for the medium.

Now it is one of the precepts of the moral life that we shall treat other human beings as ends in themselves and not as means to some other end. And there are more kinds of prostitution in this world than the sad trade which bears that name. One must feel that this whole method of approaching the other world is open to grave moral question. It is a serious matter for us to satisfy our natural curiosity or to seek solace for private grief at the expense of the stability of another human mind. There is here the peril of a grave prostitution. The moral man must satisfy himself that this method of seeking truth does not involve him in an immoral use of the agent of his quest. This seems to me the one serious objection to the methods which must be employed in this enquiry.

There is one further comment which may fitly be made upon this quest after assurance that those whom we have loved and lost awhile still live; for this is the use to which this science most naturally lends itself. The demand for such assurance always seems to me to be, in some measure, a confession that life itself, with long years of friendship and affection, has not yielded that assurance as a kind of inner certainty which needs no further proof. There is something belated in this quest for comfort, as it were a tacit confession that the years of human communion had not granted the conviction which they should have granted. I would prefer not to try to overtake, by thus plucking at the mystery, the failure of my own experience as friend and kinsman. And in the case of those whom I think I did come to know well and to love well, I would prefer to leave the matter there, with the sure memories and persuasions which experience yielded. Personally I should be very loath to seek at the hands of a medium in trance, messages from my own dear dead. I should feel that somehow I was faithless to that which they gave me and were to me in life. In short, I shrink from the implications of a furtive visit to the Cave of Endor. This may be an idiosyncrasy. I record it for what it is worth.

The scientific attempt to solve the problem of the life after death is, then, a serious adventure of the human mind, as yet not having vindicated itself. But it does involve a serious moral question which concerns the actual technique of enquiry, and in the case of the lay sitter suggests failures in the world of normal human relationships which one is reluctant to retrieve by such dubious means. Better to accept the failure and still to hope, better still the deathless certainty of Browning's *Perspice* in this experience of life with life.

When we turn from science to revelation and faith we come into another realm altogether.

There is, for Christians, first of all the fact of Easter. Without attempting to choose between the many interpretations of the fact, we are, I take it, agreed that the disciples were given on the first Easter Day assurance of the immortality of Jesus. If those experiences cannot be defined as "real," whether having their origin in the world of outer matter or of inner consciousness, then the Christian religion rests upon a gross delusion. For myself I am content to affirm, in view of the conflicting details in the Gospels, the essential reality of this experience, its witness to truth.

Granted this, one may say: The matter is then settled, there is no room for further discussion; Christ being dead yet lives, and the immortality of man is thus pledged or assured. The curious thing about this argument, however, is the fact that it carries no weight with those who do not care about Jesus and follow him. To the man who has no interest in Christianity the story of Easter is "an idle tale." It is one of the countless incredible legends which religion seems always to be weaving. It is to such a one simply "a dead hypothesis," awakening no interest or plausibility.

This difficulty, however, is inherent in the whole situation. The striking fact about the record of the Easter appearances is the very natural but too often unnoticed restriction of those appearances to the immediate company of the disciples. There is no slightest intimation that Herod or Pilate or the Roman soldiers ever "saw" Jesus again after He had been taken from the cross and laid away in the rock-hewn tomb. We are left on Friday with two or three women and one beloved disciple at the foot of the cross. When Easter dawns the figures of these women are the first figures whom we can discern, and they were the first to see the Risen Lord. Then the disciples, one after another, singly or in pairs, then the eleven, then all the brethren, perhaps five hundred, see Him.

There is here a clear suggestion that some fitness or insight on the part of men determined who should "see" Him and who should not. This, after all, is what we should expect. The whole content of Easter belongs to the subtle world of religion, and not to the cruder world of material proof. You cannot leave the rest of the Gospels in the keeping of religion, but transfer Easter to the keeping of the physical sciences. Easter, supremely, belongs in the keeping of religion. And that means that it calls for the coöperation, the insight, and expectant attitude which are always the human contribution to that mystery which we term "revelation." "Revelations" are given to persons who on the human side have fulfilled their part in the commerce of the spirit. This means, simply, that those who had really loved and followed Jesus knew His deathless life, but that to others no such certitude was given or could be given. What was true then is true now.

Quite clearly, then, the persuasion of the immortality of Jesus is not something to be proved by balancing evidence or weighing records, in an attitude of disinterested indifference. What most of us believe about that supreme affirmation we believe as the maturing conviction of our own efforts to live a Christian life, and our discovery in experience of the nature and character of Christ. We do not believe in Him because He strikes us blind with some incredible magic, we believe in the reality of all that Easter records because the life of discipleship matures in some such conclusion.

The revelation of the Christian hope, then, in so far as we are to receive it, is determined by the quality of our own discipleship. It calls for the insight of human devotion as the condition for its bestowal. Again, what was true on the first Easter Day is still true, and there is no other way to any acceptance of its truth save the way of long and faithful following after Him.

Let me turn, now, to two or three concluding considerations which, on our human side, do buttress our whole faith in the life after death and give it a reasonableness which dignifies and confirms our native hope.

There is, first of all, the moral struggle, and the inequality of human circumstance, amounting apparently to injustice. Kant was accustomed to say that if justice is not done, the whole foundations of being are removed. Science claims that justice is always done. "The ledgers of the Almighty," says Huxley, "are strictly kept and every one of us has the balance of his operations paid over to him at the end of every minute of his existence." This dogma is undoubtedly true, and yet it calls for much interpretation. In particular any such dogma of the inerrant justice of things demands that man shall be set in his whole social *milieu,* both as to heredity and environment. The problem of evil, and likewise the equally difficult but none the less baffling problem of good, is insoluble on the basis of any individualist ethic. We suffer for the mistakes and sins of others as we profit undeservedly by their labors and sacrifices. There is a kind of total justice in the experience of the race, which no one questions. But it is never possible to close and balance the account of the individual with the race and with the moral order. Too many items are still unknown and outstanding. The ethical problem raised and stated so poignantly in the book of Job defies all solution if the single individual be treated as a self-sufficient moral entity. The deeper insight of the New Testament substitutes for this incredible individualism its truer doctrine of the "members" and its world of penalty and grace in the whole experience of man in the life of the race.

But even so, a full sense of a final justice demands

that these mysteries, with all the unknown factors in experience, be made plain to the single man. It may comfort me to know that though I perish truth abides and goodness wins the day. But it cannot be a perfect triumph for me unless somehow I am conscious of the day of victory and share in it. A passionate conviction as to the triumph of good in the moral order demands that those who have fought the good fight, who have suffered in that fight and who have gone down still fighting when the cause was not yet won, should know and should share in the final victory. Less than this is less than justice and less than perfect goodness. The argument from moral experience confirms us in our faith that the moral man must know himself the final victor over his world. This knowledge in its fullness is never given to him in the present life. If it comes it can come only in a life after death.

There is, in the next place, the persuasion as to the meaning and the value of life yielded by living. We are faithful to the deeper wisdom of experience if we say that persons are the most precious realities in the world and that the development of personality through its contacts with other persons seems to be the intention and meaning of the life-process.

This judgment upon the meaning and value of life is at once a platitude and a profound truth. It is a platitude to those who take their world of men for granted. It is a truth to those who have learned by sincere and costly experience what matters most. What really matters to us in the end is our world of men. The hardest blow which the world can deal us is the blow of sorrow, the loss of those who are near and dear to us.

The poignancy of the fact of death lies not so much

in work laid down before it is completed, or in the moral struggle relinquished before the victory is won, but in the interruption of friendship and affection. The deeper cry at the grave's edge is not the cry of a thwarted moral sense, but of a desolated heart.

Now living is simply a business of drawing nearer to other human beings or of drawing apart from them. We are penned in by the bars of individuality. We struggle to let down those bars, or to get past them and into other lives. Often we are thrown back into our solitary selves. But again and again we seem to get at our fellows with a kind of immediacy, and those hours when we find our true and whole self in the world of persons around us are the best hours in living.

There is again, here, something which calls for further fulfilment. These experiences are prophetic of a fuller and larger personal life. Unless the whole content of life is a chaos and a delusion, discovering no intention or end, and discouraging honest thought, we must hold that in the world of persons and the enlargement of personal life through friendship and affection we have a clue which warrants us to think on into a life more fully personal. The alternative to such projection of immediate experience into the future is sheer irrationality. Neither the eternal hills nor the precious gems and gold of the earth are to be considered in durability and worth beside the tough and precious world where "heart speaks to heart."

For that is the religious verdict upon the meaning and value of living. And when John Henry Newman was made Cardinal he chose those words as the motto for his arms, "Cor ad cor loquitur." No other verdict upon experience or insight into living yields as much truth in the test of years as this. And if we follow Browning in his wholesome judgment, "Be sure that God ne'er dooms to waste the strength He deigns impart," we must find in this deathless power of the human heart to claim its own some pledge of that power's full occasion and opportunity. Less than this is to make a mock of the love of man for woman and the love of man for man, passing the love of woman. It is to give the lie to life itself and the yield of living. Life here, then, is an experimental adventure in the escape from the solitude of individuality and in the discovery of the true self in union with other persons. Unless this life is an irrational and cruel joke this quest creates both the demand for its own fulfilment in some other world, and the hopeful assurance of that fulfilment.

These considerations bring us on to the gospel of "the eternal moment." The modern doctrine of immortality, as I see it, is the assertion of the deathless quality of certain experiences given us here and now, and not merely a dreary perpetuity for the monotonous drudgery of our lesser hours. George Tyrrell has pointed out the fact that the indefinite and infinite extension of the humdrum life of every day is, for the Buddhist, a vision not of heaven but of hell. And Horace Bushnell once said of the preparation of an Easter sermon, that the idea of immortality too often awakens no response in our minds because it is presented as the mere dreary prolongation of our common earthly life. This idea, he said, does not and cannot awaken enthusiasm and desire. What is demanded in our thought of heaven is a qualitative difference; not longer life but another kind of life.

There is a sentence in Aristotle's metaphysics which

affirms that "Our rare best moments are like the life of God." This is, of course, the doctrine of immortality found in the fourth Gospel. Eternal Life, as conceived in that Gospel, is not a matter of life after death merely, but rather a distinction in the levels of all living here or hereafter. According to that Gospel we do not have to wait until we are dead to become immortal. We may enter into eternal life here and now. For those times and occasions of major worth in our present living, when we are at one with God and man, are in themselves eternal. Here and now we pass out of death into life. The clock ceases to register the passage of time, the movements of its hands have no significance, because we live in some moment that seems immune from the corrosion of passing time.

This is, of course, the mystic's gospel of immortality. It seems to me to be, again, a clue as to the truth. We do have certain experiences which are qualitatively lifted above the discontent of our unfulfilled selves. In these experiences we feel deeply our oneness with all Being. We are a part of that which *Is*. These eternal moments come to us from time to time in the presence of the beauty of nature, in the clear vision of some truth portrayed by art, in human comradeships, in worship. These moments know their own times and seasons. But they are the hours when we live most fully and when life seems unending and indubitable. Now the whole idea of life after death concerns these present experiences of eternal life. They are what Paul might call an "earnest" of the true nature of immortality and give us immediate experience of a qualitative perfection of life. They constitute an immediate insight into the true conception of immortality.

Finally, I have one personal impression to record, coming out of these past years of experience as a pastor. It falls to the lot of every minister, as of every doctor, to go with one man after another right up to the border line between the worlds. Dr. Osler has said that "deathbeds" in themselves yield little suggestion as to what is beyond. Most men, at the very end, die quietly and all unconscious of the change. The minister has no other evidence to adduce from the actual moments of dying which he watches through. There is here a kind provision of nature which makes the actual ending of the average human life a matter of entire unconsciousness or of dulled perception.

But the minister sees many and many a human soul face the eventuality in full and clear consciousness and approach its rendezvous with death in a spirit of high courage. What remains out of my own impressions of pastoral work in this connection is a certain strong impression of an "over-soul" in man, something of spiritual energy still standing to the credit of these dead, an unexpended capacity for life which has not been exhausted.

It is said of Jesus, in the traditional phrase, that He "overcame" the grave. The figure is that of one approaching death, not with reluctance and with waning powers, but of one sweeping up to the barrier between the worlds with such momentum that He overshot the grave which marks the boundary between the worlds, carrying on into another world. It is like a great wave that rolls up on a beach sweeping high above the mean level high-water mark.

Many men and women, in dying, have left with me, their minister, this strong suggestion of "overcoming" the grave. I have felt that although disease or accident or age have seemed to win a temporary victory, these persons came up to their end with a resilience, a capacity for experience still unexhausted. They have given the clear suggestion of an inner and spiritual life that had not worn itself out. The principle and power of true life was still theirs. They were vital, active, affectionate, hopeful. I cannot think of them as dead, because I must believe in some principle of conservation of energy and value in the universe. I must believe that energy undergoing degradation here is conserved and reincarnated elsewhere. What seems to be their loss here I must still carry on, in confident imagination, to their credit and capacity for living in another world.

This pastoral persuasion, again and again renewed, until it has deepened into a conviction with me, I give you for what it is worth. The margins of the over-soul in the nature and character of good men dead, I must believe to be still at their use and hand elsewhere. There is still something left in the impression which these persons have made upon me, which creates in my thought of them that other world which gives their unspent strength and goodness its new occasion. This is not formal logic. It is, rather, one of those yields of a particular type of experience which has issued in "a passionate intuition." You may match it with your own persuasion as to men of strength and virtue who have passed out of your own world.

For the life of daily discipleship, then, there is no scientific proof of immortality. There is only the practice of immortal life in the unremitting moral struggle, in the world of persons seeking the true self of each and all, in the chance eternal moment, and in the witness of those who being dead yet live in our memory and hope. Being a Christian yields such conviction as to Jesus. And the whole essence of Christianity is its assurance that what is true of Jesus is the ultimate truth of all human life.

THE FUNCTION OF THE CHURCH IN MODERN SOCIETY

CHARLES W. GILKEY

Pastor of Hyde Park Baptist Church, Chicago.

CHAPTER VIII

THE FUNCTION OF THE CHURCH IN MODERN SOCIETY

CHARLES W. GILKEY

SIGNS are not wanting that the attitude of many serious-minded modern men toward the Church, as toward religion in general, is beginning to change from one of criticism, or at best of indifference, to one of interested and often of sympathetic reconstruction. We have just come through a period when it has been the fashion everywhere to charge the Church with even more than her admittedly lengthy debit account of sins of omission and commission great and small: no editor, scholar, speaker, cartoonist, paragraph-writer, or even up-to-date preacher so blind as to do her reverence, and none so humble as to hesitate to tell her what she must do to save herself from impending shipwreck and abandonment on the sands of time. In an inimitable essay on "Heckling the Church" in the *Atlantic Monthly* for December, 1911, Dr. H. E. Fosdick said:

> A perusal of current literature in reference to the church reveals how much the rage it has become to censure the blunders of organized religion. There are fashions in magazine articles as well as in dress, and the present vogue is, by any means, to drub the church. Recent essays in which, with force and cleverness, both friends and foes have pointedly remarked upon ecclesiastical failures . . . leave the impression, not only that there are grievous errors to be criticized, but that some people are having rare sport criticizing them.

But since these words were written, many things have changed; among them certainly, to some extent at least, the position of the Church in public opinion and regard. Dr. Fosdick's point in this article—that the Church, as a very human institution, reveals the same common faults of our human nature that equally appear in our politics, our industry, and our education—has been given further emphasis by the Great War, with its relentless revelation of these weaknesses as running through our entire social order. In fact, the balance has swung the least bit back the other way. America's participation in the Great War, requiring as it did the prompt development of an intelligent and tenacious morale throughout the nation, showed the Church only less valuable than the press as an instrument for broadcasting information and appeal, and superior to any other agency in its moral authority and dynamic. So well have our civic and humanitarian enterprises learned this lesson, that nowadays a minister's office hours and daily mail are alike burdened with appeals to serve as publicity man for all kinds of good causes; and if he follow every philanthropic prescription for the subject of his next Sunday's sermon, he will (as Dean Sperry also has pointedly observed in the *Atlantic*) have scarcely a Sunday in the year free on which to preach the gospel!

For, as this situation clearly indicated, the Church has actually begun to awaken to some at least of her responsibilities: so suddenly, in fact, that to some of her present-day critics she seems to be moving very incalculably and sometimes not quite sanely, like one who has just opened his eyes without yet recovering all his senses. It was only a decade ago that we heard much from labor leaders about the great gulf between the Church and the workingman, created by her failure to understand social wrongs and hopes, and by her complete financial dependence upon the prosperous whose gifts were usually as ill made as their gains were ill gotten. But (however it may still be between the Church and the workingman) much of the social criticism of the Church has, since the steel strike of 1919, come from quite the other side, on the ground that she has become far too radical for many of her supporters: much more is heard to-day about the rich reactionaries who are canceling their subscriptions as a protest, than about their tainted support of a class institution.

But he who listens carefully to these contemporary solicitations and criticisms of the Church will easily detect under them the same note of social anxiety that sounds so often in modern life. In this chaotic, disintegrating world into which the War has carried us, the Church is asked to be the custodian of many treasures beside her own pearl of great price. Mr. Babson calls on far-sighted business men to support her as a kind of universal moral fidelity and casualty assurance society. Mr. Wells finds the salvaging of civilization, and Lord Bryce the future of democracy, somehow bound up with the future of religion. Sir Philip Gibbs, scanning the horizon for signs of social hope, sees the brightest prospect in the direction of historic Christianity. The British delegation goes home from Versailles, the British prime minister from repeated breakdowns in European conferences, the Japanese ambassador even from the Washington Conference, saying that the future hopes of men rest with religion. General Pershing is even more explicit, and also President

Harding: the prevention of war, says the one, the stability of society, says the other, depends ultimately upon religion as organized in the Church.

The honest churchman may not be at all sure that the Church is yet ready to carry easily such large responsibilities as these. He looks over at the Fundamentalist brother in a neighboring pew, and the heresy-hunter in a sister church; he reads the headlines of new theological controversy in the metropolitan press; he notes the apparent resurgence since the war of irreconcilable denominationalism in religion as well as irreconcilable nationalism in politics; he watches the tiny trickle of strong men entering the ministry, and the swelling stream of those who are leaving it; he puzzles and grieves over the slowness of the Church to sense the things that pertain to the world's peace, and to proclaim them from the housetops as part of the gospel of Him at whose birth the tidings came, "Peace on earth to men of goodwill." And yet withal he is encouraged: by the conspicuous influence of the American churches in bringing about the Washington Conference; by the new spirit moving in every great religious body; by the great expansion of missionary intelligence and interest as well as of benevolent giving; by the better understanding that is steadily strengthening between religious, social, and educational leaders; and not least, by the response of the younger generation, and the quality if not the quantity of the younger ministry. The president of the University of Chicago came home from the Northern Baptist Convention at Indianapolis last June to say that the most heartening thing he had seen in years was not simply the unexpectedly complete victory of the spirit of tolerance and progress over intolerance and reaction at what may well prove a turning point in American religious history; but even more the spirit and quality of the younger men in the ministry that had made that victory possible. The whole situation of the Church to-day, with its great opportunities and its obvious limitations, reminds one of that superb word of Paul, "A great door and effectual is opened unto me, and there are many adversaries."

At such a time it is appropriate to face afresh the question of the function of the Church in human society, and to attempt to restate the reasons which justify her support and guarantee her future as a permanent necessity among human beings endowed and organized as we are, and as our children will be after us. Especially is it timely, thus early in the new age into which modern science and industry and the modern social conscience have combined to lead us, to ask what special service the Church may render, and what peculiar opportunities and responsibilities confront her, in the characteristic conditions of the age in which we live. Our subject falls naturally, therefore, into two parts: one dealing with the permanent functions of the Church in human life, the other with her contemporary tasks in our modern time.

It should be said also that in thus thinking of the Church we do not assume any presuppositions, historical or theological, as to what the Church is or ought to be, and that we do not use the word itself in any esoteric or technical sense. Questions of history, polity, and doctrine, that have bulked so large in most discussions of this subject, we waive entirely: important as they may be in other connections, they surely yield in urgency to the previous question which is on the lips of so many and in the hearts of more to-day: Whatever the Church's past, what can she do in the living present, and has she any future? What we mean by the Church is what ordinary man means when he asks these questions—a social group formed by the union of individual Christians for common worship and service. Whether this group be an informal company of Christians seeking fellowship with each other and with God through Jesus Christ, or an organized local congregation federated with other such local groups into a denomination, or whether it thinks of itself as a single national or international organization that is supreme over its local branches, matters not for our present purpose. It does matter, however, that we should remember that we are considering, not the fortunes or functions of religion in general, but those of the social institution which it has created for its own cultivation. That religion is a permanent element in human nature and life may perhaps fairly be taken for granted among men who think on these things, and is assumed in this article. It is at least conceivable, however, as the theory of some radical Protestants seem to be, and as the practice of very many lukewarm church members seems to imply, that, while religion may abide, the Church has outlived its usefulness. Whether this is actually the case is precisely our question.

I. *Permanent Functions of the Church in Human Life.*

In view of this social interdependence of all our higher life, the indispensable function of the Church as a permanent necessity and support of the spiritual interests of human society becomes evident. As by combining the limited strength or wisdom or capital of many individuals into an army or a council or a corporation, a collective achievement is made possible which no single person could have attempted; and as within such a social group standards of efficiency and attainment are maintained to which many of the weaker would not individually attain alone, so may a group of people with moral aspirations and Christian purposes pool, so to speak, their spiritual capital in a church, and draw on this common spiritual stock for support in times of their personal religious doubt or obscurity, or moral strain. That such spiritual support from the common capital is a reality, let the experience of all who have found help in the public worship of the Church at times of individual need, or who have felt the steadying power of the Christian public opinion of the Church at times of moral strain, bear abundant witness.

The number of us who at some time or other are kept from religious "backsliding" or moral lapse by the sustaining power of public opinion is perhaps, if we only knew, larger than we should like to think for the sake of the credit of individual human nature; but at least it shows how powerful and indispensable are the social sanctions that hold us in our proper places. The human universe, like the solar system and the whole cosmos of which it is a part, is held in place and swung in orderly and dependable orbit by the influence of its individual members on each other; gravitation is in this sense a spiritual as well as a physical force—and in both realms is fundamental and essential. The Church, in other words, has as its first permanent function in human life the support of the otherwise morally and religiously insufficient individual in his higher life.

In this sense, social and psychological rather than dogmatic, the Church may fairly be called an "ark of salvation" for struggling individual swimmers on the sea of spiritual experience.

A second aspect of the Church's function is closely related to this first. Not simply is the moral and religious life of most men supported and stimulated by the common spiritual life of the Church; it is very often itself originated as an offspring from that life more or less directly. For it is true of spiritual life as of physical, that it springs from previous life; religious experience is quickened in one soul by and from the experience of others, and moral resolve is fired by the example or exhortation of an inspiring character. Now while it is true that this creative contact of personalities is not seldom a matter of direct personal influence ("personal work" is the traditional phrase) in which the Church as such has no share, it is also true that a great many people are not themselves directly in touch with any spiritually quickening personality of this sort, and can come into such life-giving contact only through the Church in which such personalities gather and are accessible. And not only so, but the Church herself, like any social organization, develops a corporate life of her own that is different from, and stronger than, the lives of her members individually or even in the aggregate. The "life of the Church" is a very real spiritual entity, as every live member of a living church knows. And this common or corporate life is often as potent as any individual influence to beget new life in others. It is no accident that conversions usually take place in churches or as a direct result of church work, and at special times and seasons of spiritual travail of the common soul. Life from life is nature's law; and the corporate as well as the individual spiritual life can bring forth and bear.

Nor is it simply contemporary life that thus has power to reproduce itself. Vital spiritual experience has an astonishing quality of timelessness—it seems never to lose the power to quicken new life from itself. The experience and example of ancient "saints, apostles, prophets, martyrs" have almost as much power of inspiration over us as over their contemporaries and successors—and in many cases even more. The "life of the Church" thus becames much more than the aggregate of its component individual lives, more even than the corporate life which all these with each other create. It includes also in a very real sense the timeless experience of all those who, "having done the will of God, abide forever," and likewise the accumulating or rather enlarging common life of the Church of all the ages. This "communion of saints" thus becomes a corporate life wider and deeper and mightier than that of any age or group, and able continually to call forth new life to reproduce and enrich itself.

Abstract and intangible as this argument may perhaps seem, it appears as by no means unreal or invalid when we consider the history and experience of all the "Catholic" churches, and their sheer power to perpetuate themselves *as institutions,* with a minimum of the personal contact of individuals which Protestantism has always magnified. Still more does it so appear when we consider the relation of the Church to that greatest but one of all Christian sources and springs of religious experience—the Bible.

The Bible as we have it is essentially a church book.

Though not written for ecclesiastical purposes, it still remains true that it was collected, transmitted, preserved, and interpreted, *in the Church.* In other words, this wonderful self-revelation of original Hebrew and Christian piety, this unique record of religious experience, has been handed down to us in and through the Church, and is a kind of visible transcript of the spiritual life which the Church has always possessed and transmitted. And as the Bible has always been like an overflowing vessel of "living water," "quick and powerful" to call forth Christian experience and stimulate Christian living in the successive generations, so has the Church ever been the channel through which has poured down through the ages the inexhaustible stream from which the vessel was originally filled.

Still more evident is this when we consider the relation which the Church has always sustained to the most powerful of all sources of Christian life and experience—the person of Jesus Christ. In His presence, in contact with His personality as it stands forth in the Gospels, the essential Christian experience is most steadily and surely produced: there God becomes real and fatherly and trustworthy, life becomes big with meaning and the promise of immortality, and the kingdom of heaven becomes a present task and a future hope. Now it is *within the Church* that His memory, His portrait, His teachings, His spirit, have been kept alive; it is "where two or three are gathered together" in His name, that He is "in the midst." Historically speaking, it was within the Church that the sayings of Jesus were first collected and treasured, and His biographies written, and there that through all the centuries since, however inadequately or distortedly at times, He has been "lifted up" to the homage and obedience and imitation of mankind. Surely not least among the age-long services of the Church has been this: that it has held up before mankind steadily the most important figure in human history. And this remains in our time a permanent and indispensable function of the Church—for our age needs the vision of Christ certainly not less than those that have gone before. And so long as the Church, by its preaching and teaching and witness-bearing, thrusts the figure of Christ before the attention of men, not only in the sanctuary, but in the market-place, the school and the home, so long it is meeting the condition on which depends the contemporary fulfilment of His own ancient and oft-verified promise, "I, if I be lifted up, will draw all men unto me."

In other words, the orthodox Catholic doctrine of the Church as the repository and guardian of an authoritative tradition is simply, as dogmas so often are, the theological perversion and intellectual incrustation of a spiritual experience. It is not *tradition* which the Church ought to treasure up and transmit, but *life*—spiritual life. She becomes a channel through which the stream of Christian experience pours itself on down through the centuries, enriching itself and quickening new life as it goes. The Bergsonian philosophy, with its vivid and stimulating picture of life as a movement thrusting itself forward through real time into ever new and unforeseen individual manifestations, may help us moderns to make more real to ourselves this conception of the age-long life of the Church, and its relation to the individual lives of contemporary Christians who are quickened by, or spring from it. The second permanent function of the Church is thus the transmission from generation to generation of Christian life and experience in all its quickening power, and especially of those life-giving and never failing spiritual experiences which the Church has made accessible to the world in the Bible and in the person of Jesus Christ.

A third aspect of the permanent function of the Church in human life appears when we consider the true relation of religion to the common affairs and routine of daily living in the average community. In time past, and in some types of Christianity to-day, religion has been apparently conceived as an occasional mysterious transaction or ritual act, which takes place at some special revival season or at some central and consecrated place, and by which the Divine is brought down into our human world to be adored and appropriated. It is the descent of God within the reach of man. For all real Protestants, however, religion is no occasional transaction or rare ecstasy, but an ever renewed experience, attained through prayer and meditation and daily duty-doing and unselfish service, of the presence of the Divine in our hearts and lives in the midst of the affairs of every day. It is "the life of God in the soul of man"—in whose transfiguring light nothing can be secular save what is sinful, and in whose purifying presence nothing worthy can remain common or unclean.

At the same time, however, as we have seen, the average individual requires some social support, some objective and organized meditation, before he can catch and keep this divine presence within him. And particularly is this true where the pressure of life's daily round and common task is forever tending to conceal or to extinguish the light within. In this regard the Church serves as a kind of constant conductor of the divine life and presence into the midst of every community, and into the heart of every member. Not simply at some central shrine, but into the midst of every least community where "two or three are gathered together," she brings the common vision of Christ, the common experience of God. No spot on earth where two souls can meet for worship is so isolated, no house is so humble or service so barren or preacher so ill equipped or poor, as to miss this spiritual blessing if only the seeking be sincere; and by this blessing the common life and labor of these seekers and that community may be lit up with the very presence of God. And this sanctifying and transfiguring ministry of the Church is not simply universal, but also constantly recurrent. Were it only once a month or once a year, the fire might languish and die in the long intervals. But once or twice or thrice a week the social bond is renewed, the common aspiration is lifted, the common blessing comes. It is as important that this social mediation of religion should be constantly repeated so as to touch and transfigure the constantly renewed and ever fresh pulses or periods of time that, as Bergson reminds us, make up life, as that it should touch every least and last locality where men live together.

We may perhaps illustrate this third aspect of the function of the Church by the analogy of the production of steam. A ritualistic or revivalistic religion, like the old-fashioned boiler, brings the divine fire down to the outside of the undifferentiated mass of human life, and by the application of its heat there seeks to generate power. But the mass is slow to penetrate and stubborn to transform by any such purely external method. It is the function of the Church to serve as the intricate system of channels in the modern tubular boiler, each local church acting as a single tube and all together carrying the divine fire straight to the heart and out through all the ranges of human life, till spiritual power is generated everywhere at once. Only so can the kingdom come in all parts and at all times of our human experience. It is thus the third function of the Church to relate religion vitally to the ordinary life of all sorts and conditions of men, at all times and places of their existence.

A fourth aspect of the function of the Church in human life can perhaps be stated more simply and directly than the three thus far considered. It is that a task so vast and intricate as that to which Christianity summons its followers—the bringing in on earth of God's kingdom and the doing of His will among men—can be adequately attempted, much less accomplished, only by an organized society. All the considerations of efficiency which have led to the modern elaboration of organization in all departments of life require a like measure of organized efficiency on the part of the Church if she is to accomplish her task; and in proportion as her task is vaster, more delicate, and more difficult than that of manufacturing and marketing a commercial product, or administering a city or a state, or waging a war, must her organization be not less but more efficient. The necessity of a permanent machinery that shall survive the individual fortunes of short-lived mortals; of a division of labor that shall assign each member to the tasks that he can best perform; of a central administration that shall eliminate waste and duplication, and bring her full resources to bear on the most important tasks in hand; and of a constant supervision and training that shall increase the efficiency of each worker; these necessities of every undertaking that would accomplish great things through human instrumentality are laid upon the Church as well.

But there remains a yet deeper reason why the Christian task can be adequately attempted only by a society; a reason which our High-Church friends have been far quicker to see and appropriate than we still individualistic "sectarians." It is, briefly, that the Christian ideal for human life is a social ideal, the Christian gospel a social gospel; and that therefore this ideal can be realized, this gospel effectively preached, only through a *society.* If it be true, as we certainly think it is, that our present social order is fundamentally un-Christian, and that our Christian task is not finished until it as well as the individuals who compose it be redeemed, and the "environment evangelized" as well as the souls that are constantly exposed to its influence; then, by the same fundamental logic that makes it impossible that a man drowning out of reach of shore or boat should be rescued by anyone who cannot swim himself, or that an attacking fleet should ever be captured or destroyed by a defending army, it follows that this social task requires a social instrument, a *Church,* for its achievement. Just as in any highly organized sport a number of picked-up individuals, however brilliant, can hardly hope to defeat a real "team," so no mere aggregation of individuals, however saintly, can hope to overcome the "kingdoms of this world" and make them "the kingdoms of our

Lord and of his Christ." As a means to the establishment of an era of brotherhood and justice and mutual service, we must have a Church that is founded on, and characterized by, these same fundamental Christian principles: no other type of Church can ever achieve the kingdom, nor can it be achieved without any church at all. The fourth permanent function of the Church is therefore a coöperative attempt to realize an essentially social ideal.

It will be observed that these four functions are after all simply various aspects of what is fundamentally a single or at most a two-sided fact—the social nature of all human life, and the correspondingly inevitable social character of all religion and notably of the Christian religion. From this elemental fact follows directly the permanent necessity of the Church in human life; and all analyses or elaborations of its functions (of which many more might be made) and all analogies of its working (of which those above are offered as suggestive merely) are really only recognitions from various approaches of the ultimate fact that "no man liveth to himself," but that "we are all members one of another."

II. *Special Functions of the Church in Modern Society.*

While these permanent functions of the Church thus inhere in the fundamental characteristics of human life always and everywhere as we know it, and are thus the real basis of the Church's abiding destiny, it is also true that in any age there may be special conditions urgently needing just what the Church has or ought to have to give, and challenging her to press with special vigor one or another of these functions, or even to add to them others that the needs of the times or the nature of her own ideals demand. That this is notably true of our own time, that the Church is to-day facing at once a serious crisis and a great opportunity, has become a commonplace. Indeed, there is danger that the very recognition of our peculiar modern situation may lead us to an overemphasis on the differences between our own time and earlier ages, and to an obscuring of the permanent needs of human life which the Church, now as always, must meet. The modern man is after all not so different at heart from his ancestors as some very up-to-date thinkers would have us believe. The modern world greatly needs to ponder the dictum of Goethe—"Mankind is forever advancing, but man remains ever the same"—and the modern Church, in her eagerness to meet the new needs of mankind, must not cease to minister to the perennial needs of man.

At the same time, there is no doubt that the Church is facing in our time a situation, fraught at once with crisis and with opportunity, such as rarely in her history she has had to meet. It has become trite to say that "conditions have changed," so that her traditional methods of doing the very work which we have insisted is her permanent function are no longer effective, and that she must either find new methods or leave her essential task undone. This is unquestionably true. But further it is also true that certain temporary functions which, under the peculiar exigencies of past ages, she then assumed because no one else was doing them, and because they were related to her own ideals, have since been taken over by other agencies created for the purpose, leaving her without the prestige which once these activities brought her. As everybody knows, she has thus handed over education to public schools and private colleges, eleemosynary work very largely to charitable organizations and to the state, and direct social reform to political parties. And yet once more: it is also true that certain characteristic changes in our modern life have deeply affected her work and considerably increased its present difficulty. Modern science, philosophy, and historical scholarship have completely changed men's ideas of the universe and of their own relation to it, and have modified profoundly the form, if not the substance, of all religious teaching. Out of the resulting period of theological transition and religious confusion we have by no means passed. And the increased complexity and high tension of modern life have made it increasingly difficult for the Church to get the ear of men, and to find sufficient opportunities to exercise to any perceptible extent an influence which must be as delicate and subtle as hers.

But these facts, as at least the younger generation of our time are beginning to recognize, constitute a challenge to advance rather than an excuse for retreat. They call for aggressive leadership to discover new methods of doing these perennial tasks in the midst of a new age. They require constructive thinking to restate the ancient truths of Christianity in such new forms as to command even modern attention. And no less do they demand a realignment of our forces: the withdrawal of our energies from certain points of assured victory on humanity's wide battlefield where we are no longer so much needed; the concentration of our forces at certain newly crucial points where the issue is still doubtful; or the seizing of some vantage points where the fighting has hardly yet begun. If there were special opportunities for service in previous ages where the Church could win great prestige and strike mighty blows for the advance of the kingdom, by espousing causes and upholding interests which others were leaving to defeat, surely there must be such special opportunities in an age so tossed in tradition and torn with conflict as our own. Are there such, and if so, what are they? That is our second great question.

The first great opportunity and challenge offered to the Church by distinctly modern conditions grows out of the new industrialism into which the last century has carried us. The development of machinery and of the factory system, the division of labor, the concentration into cities, and, above all, the enormous increase in the volume of our American wealth due to the exploitation of our unrivaled natural resources, have combined to emphasize business standards of success until they have become the accepted standards for the measurement of values of all kinds among us; and commercialism has come in upon us like a flood. The absence of a leisure class and of a landed aristocracy, with their traditions, has favored this process. Prosperity rather than human welfare has become our national ideal, all things material or immaterial are estimated in terms of money value or cost (witness our newspaper headlines which describe everything from building sites to paintings and opera singers by a figure with a $ before it), and we tremble to take any great forward step in social progress for fear of its possible effects on business and profits. The rich are our national heroes of success, our aristocracy is one chiefly of wealth, and the eyes of all of us are focused on money making as the one universally recognized road to recognition—for a man is known among us by the money he has made. A keen observer recently remarked that as a nation we were working all day to make money and then sitting up half the night to spend it—and that this seemed to be all there was to most of our personal lives. Small wonder is it that rich and poor among us have had their standards frightfully externalized, their sense for things unseen and eternal deadened, and their unresponsiveness to spiritual interests greatly increased, by this all-invading commercialism. The marked reaction of the last few years against all this has come none too soon, and may well go much farther before the balance is restored in our national life between material and spiritual interests.

The attention given to things spiritual in our national life is further lessened by the marked speeding up of the pace of modern living. In some industries the standard pace of labor has, by means of speeding up the machinery, been actually doubled by count in the last few years. The distinguished economist in charge of the Pittsburgh Survey reported: "The mass of workers in the steel industry are driven as large numbers of laborers, whether slave or free, have scarcely before in human industry been driven." And this speeding up has been felt all through our modern life, in our leisure and our amusements (witness the effects of the automobile) hardly less than in our industries. The result has been to make it increasingly difficult to get the attention of people—particularly the continuous attention. Nor is this to be wondered at when we remember how jaded this pace of modern life must leave nerves and minds and bodies that have been driven all the working-day at this high speed. Busy men, and women too for that matter, are very often too tired in the evening for anything but the lightest reading or the most trivial amusement, and on Sunday for anything but a trip into the country. This increased pace of modern life, instead of leaving more leisure for higher interests, is thus making it more and more difficult to fasten the attention of busy men on anything serious outside that which occupies their working hours.

In such a largely commercialized and highly driven life, it is perhaps more than ever in human history an all-important function of the Church to witness to the reality and power of things unseen and eternal, and to make the busy modern man, whether capitalist or laborer, realize their supreme importance. She must insist that it profits neither a man nor a nation anything to gain the whole world and lose its own soul; that a man's or a nation's life consisteth not in the abundance of the things which it possesseth; that it is not the will of our Father in heaven that one of His little ones, whether overworked in cotton mills, or stifled in tenements, or starved in poverty, or corrupted with vice, should perish; that the moral order and an eternal destiny and God are the ultimate and supreme realities of existence. The Church must deliver herself from the insidious taint of commercialism, and fight uncompromisingly against the worship and service of Mammon wherever it appears. She must make conscience, both individual and social, vocal and authoritative in the lives and affairs of men and of communities. She must open to driven and distraught souls, out of the possible gloomy treadmill of their daily life, a window toward heaven. In short, she must recognize it as a part of her distinctive modern task, by insisting on the infinite worth of the individual and the eternal values of brotherly human relationships, to "spiritualize democracy"; for if democracy is not spiritualized, it may too easily become a vast social machine for greater economic efficiency and greater personal gratification. The social possibilities opening before a truly spiritualized democracy are tremendous; but a commercialized aristocracy and a brutalized proletariat would make up a society that in the long run could produce and exalt little but mediocrity, superficiality, and frivolity. Away from such perils and toward such possibilities of democracy it is the present duty of the Church to lead our modern life.

A second special opportunity for the Church in our age and nation grows out of the fact that we Americans are as a people deeply individualistic. It is one of the main secrets of our national strength and achievement that we have been so; and all the conditions of our pioneer history have tended to accentuate this national characteristic. But now that the pioneer stage of our development is largely past, and the industrial era is full upon us, it is absolutely essential, not only for our future attainments, but also for our future salvation as a people, that we should outgrow the individualism of our national youth wherein it was "every man for himself and the devil take the hindermost," and enter into the brotherly coöperation of maturity wherein we shall all recognize and act on the principle that we are all "members one of another." This is, of course, not socialism in the economic or political sense; it is socialism only in the sense of the organic unity of society in which Christianity is fundamentally socialistic, and every developed nation must also be if it is to survive.

Now it is surely one of the most hopeful auguries of our national future that this sense of our organic unity, which is at least the first stage of a growing sense of brotherhood, is increasing so rapidly among us; that a social conscience is developing which feels keenly the burden of our national sins and shortcomings and will not rest satisfied till they are overcome; and that a common will is asserting itself which alone can carry us forward as a united democracy on the path of social progress.

But hopeful as are these beginnings, we yet have far to go. The forces of reactionary individualism are still mighty among us, and have on their side, not only the settled social habits and institutions of generations, but also the letter and even sometimes the spirit of our system of laws and our written constitutions. The rapid tendency to class stratification and increased class tension among us as the glaringly unequal distribution of wealth increases at a pace accelerated by our enormously enlarging production of wealth, and the emergence among our increasingly heterogeneous population of strong racial cleavages and antipathies, are centrifugal social forces which must be counteracted and overcome by stronger centripetal forces of social cohesion and brotherhood, if we are to survive as a democracy.

Further, the social agencies which we have so far developed exist chiefly either for their own self-seeking (as in the case of labor unions, commercial organizations, and fraternal orders) or for some specific piece of social betterment (as with our societies for particular philanthropic and charitable purposes or for special objects of reform). In other words, while we are organizing rapidly into more or less sharply competing groups, each for mutual benefit within itself, and while we are attending admirably to the achievement of specific reforms as the need for them appears, we are leaving the general social sense and conscience among us to develop by itself without definite cultivation. That it does develop as a by-product of these specific social strivings is undoubted; that in these modern days God is causing it to spring forth and grow among us, "we know not how," some of us firmly believe. But is it not also plain that the development of the social sense and conscience in general, the deepening of the realization that we human beings and we American fellow citizens are really "members one of another," cannot be left to chance, to incidental by-production, or even to a kind Providence, if our social perils are to be averted and our social possibilities as the world's great experiment in democracy are to be realized?

It is this same problem in its international even more than in its social aspect which the War has made the very crux of our civilization. For the first time in human history thoughtful men are putting the question whether our civilization may not perish by the very instruments it had created for its self-defense,—like Saul falling on his own sword. Every man who thinks fundamentally on that great issue of the New Year and the coming years works through, from whatever approach, to the same central conclusion, that the only solution is the spread of the "international mind"—and heart. Thus slowly and laboriously—and at such cost—do we discover in experience the truth of the angels' promise "Peace on earth—to men of good will."

Now what has been not only the mission but the achievement of Christianity from its very beginning to create such international-mindedness? Paul reported its early success when he wrote to the Colossians: "Where there is neither Greek nor Jew, . . . Barbarian, Scythian, bond nor free." From that day to this the Christian Church has in some real sense transcended all bonds of race and station, till it is to-day the most international as well as the most democratic of human associations. And the modern missionary enterprise, with all its inadequacies, is a world-wide school of international-mindedness on the highest levels of human intercourse. Wherever at a country cross-road the missionary sewing circle meets (no matter how provincial their gossip as they sew), their spiritual horizon is being stretched beyond the oceans: wherever children bring their pennies to Sunday school to keep the little Russians and Armenians alive, a sense of interest and responsibility is being formed that will bear its fruit in the international relationships of the next generation. If the seeds of present war were sown generations ago, the seeds of future peace must be planted now. And the world-wide Christian Church is doing just that.

Here, then is the second and perhaps the supreme opportunity of the Church in the peculiar conditions of modern life—to cultivate and sensitize the social conscience. She alone among all our human institutions exists for the specific purpose of making men realize that they are all brothers, children of a common Father in one great human family. Her public worship in itself is or ought to be a tremendous force working for this end; intercessory prayers for the special needs of "all sorts and conditions of men" must stir in the heart and conscience of every true worshiper, in the most searching and appropriate way that human experience knows, the realization of human brotherhood in common dependence upon God; sermons, if they be in any true sense prophetic, must arouse the social conscience, and exalt the common weal, and utter forth again the ancient summons of Christianity to individual repentance for the sake of the general good—"change your life, for God is introducing among men a new order." And all the Church's work and "labor of love," ameliorative, redemptive, missionary, tends or ought to tend to deepen this sense of brotherhood to the ends of the earth. That the Church often fails in this divine mission, that her social service is sometimes neutralized by her own too frequent unbrotherliness, is no refutation of her function, but rather an evidence both of its importance and of its difficulties. She is herald and ambassador—and most of all the ministering servant—of that kingdom of God which is "not meat and drink, but righteousness and peace and joy in the divine Spirit."

And this leads directly and specifically to the third great opportunity of the Church in the modern age—the definite promotion of the common welfare at the next point to be gained. In previous ages the Church has not been slow to undertake specific tasks which she saw lay along the pathway to her spiritual ideals, and which others were not undertaking. Thus in ancient times she undertook the whole work of relieving the poor and caring for the sick and disabled, which in our more advanced stage of social evolution the state has taken over. Thus in the Dark Ages she undertook the preservation of classical literature and the cultivation of science, philosophy, music, and art. Thus in our own land she has been an indispensable pioneer in the providing of education and the establishing of law and order. But now that in the course of social development these specific tasks have been measurably completed, or taken over by other more appropriate and adequate agencies, it is for her, not to lament over lost prestige or outworn opportunities, but to press forward to meet the new needs of a new age.

That the Church has not wholly lost her ancient initiative, that she is not wholly blind to the new situation, let the whole recent development of institutional and neighborhood church work in the neediest part of the cities, of redemptive agencies for down-and-out men and unfortunate women, of activities for social outlook and uplift in the country church—let the whole intricate machinery of such efficient "arms of the Church" as the Young Men's and Young Women's Christian Associations—be at least partial evidence. Amid the spiritual darkness of Asia and Africa to-day the Church is doing exactly the same pioneering work for civilization and education and the medical relief of human suffering, which she did for Europe in the Middle Ages and for America in its earlier days. Along these lines, at home and abroad, her distinctive and immediate tasks clearly lie at the present time. It is always hers to undertake promptly such specific tasks as lie in the direction of her ideals and are not otherwise being performed.

When changing conditions, advancing social progress, or the development of more adequate and appropriate social machinery make it advisable for her to change her methods, or to turn over to others any of these temporary functions, she should do so without hesitation or discouragement—and press on to new and unoccupied points of social conflict or conquest. Even if, in the rapidly increasing complexity of our social machinery, she should at any moment find all the special social issues of the hour in the hands of organizations formed for these specific purposes, it would still be her important function to educate public opinion on these same issues, and to rally it in reinforcements that will ensure victory at the precise points where the contemporary conflict is hottest. And always, above and beyond these changing tasks of the day, will remain those permanent functions in human life which alone would justify and require her existence. The Church, in short, is or ought to be at any moment the most sensitive and responsive part of the body politic—the keenest surface of its conscience to feel the newest social danger, the strong cutting edge of its common will to press through obstacles on to higher social attainments. She is or ought to be a permanently organized force of social minute-men, ready to rush into any unexpected breach in the walls of our civilization and to hold it temporarily against the invading enemies of our human welfare until new defenses can be built; ready, too, to dart ahead and seize any commanding points of social vantage that will facilitate or protect the advance of humanity on its long march to better and higher things.

Conclusions.

It is evident that these special duties of the Church in modern life are simply concrete applications to contemporary social conditions of the permanent functions of the Church in human society which were earlier considered. This recognition raises the question whether it may be possible to summarize the entire discussion in terms of a comprehensive definition or analogy. The latter is perhaps the wiser quest to follow; since in a subject so vast and vague as this, concrete analogies that are at all accurate are often more illuminating and suggestive than any abstract definitions.

It happens that the course of social evolution has provided us with an analogy in a sphere close enough to be accurate, familiar enough to be illuminating, and practical enough to be suggestive. During the last seven centuries the colleges and universities of the modern world have become, more largely perhaps than any other institutions, the custodians of the higher life and interests of humanity. Within them the flame of pure scholarship and original research is kept alive. They train and develop thousands upon thousands of immature personalities to be worthy members in the "fellowship of educated men"—and this training is their peculiar and permanent function. But in addition they also give a partial or complete technical training for particular callings; they are constantly making new discoveries in applied science, or advancing new principles of social well-being, which are at once put to the service of society in practical life; and they are always centers and rallying-points for patriotism and public spirit. Their multitudes of alumni throughout the world look back each to his Alma Mater with a loyalty and affectionate devotion which has few if any counterparts in human life, for each man recognizes how incalculable is his debt. The alumni of each college, or of all the colleges together, are, however, only a part of that great "fellowship of educated men" of all ages and races, who are bound together by common intellectual interests, ideals, and purposes into an invisible and organized but most real society. But though the colleges do not train all these truly educated men, they are incomparably the best and surest schools in which students may qualify themselves to enter this timeless fellowship.

What the college is to the intellectual life of the world, that the Church is or ought to be to its moral and religious life. She has always kept the flame of social altruism and of spiritual devotion burning bright. Under her molding and inspiring influence pass thousands upon thousands of immature souls, to be shaped into Christian men and women—and this is her peculiar and permanent function. That so many of these are women and children is to a far-seeing eye a sign not of her weakness but of her glory and her opportunity—for these are the mothers and the members of the coming generation. But while it is the chief and central "business of the Church to make Christians," she may and ought at the same time to enlist and train and organize workers for particular social tasks, to serve society in all possible practical ways, and to take the lead in all spiritual and social advance. Her members and beneficiaries owe her a loyalty and devotion commensurate with the spiritual blessings she has conferred upon them and upon their fellows. But all the members of these visible churches are only a part of that great fellowship of spiritually- and socially-minded men of all the generations, who in their relations with each other and with God their Father constitute the invisible but most real kingdom of heaven. He who would qualify himself for entrance into that kingdom can best do so within the fellowship of the Church. For she is the spiritual Alma Mater of humanity, training men on earth for the eternal fellowship of the kingdom here and hereafter.

CHRISTIANITY AND INTERNATIONAL RELATIONS

ROBERT E. SPEER

Secretary Presbyterian Board of Foreign Missions. President Federal Council of Churches of Christ in America. Author, Lecturer, World Traveler.

CHAPTER IX

CHRISTIANITY AND INTERNATIONAL RELATIONS

ROBERT E. SPEER

SOME time ago an old friend, Professor Lang, of the University of Alabama, told me a curious incident of which he had been a witness. It occurred in the city of Edinburgh, in the winter of 1909, when Professor Lang was there taking postgraduate work in the university. One day, he said, he noticed on one of the billboards of the university the advertisement of a lecture which was to be delivered that evening in McEwen Hall, the great hall of the university, by Mr. Arthur Balfour, as he was then, on the subject, "The Moral Values Which Unite the Nations." Professor Lang said that of course he was not going to miss such an opportunity, and as early as possible he went around to the hall and got a seat in the front row of the first balcony. In the moments before the lecture began, he looked about over the audience and saw sitting immediately opposite him on the front row of the balcony on the other side a Japanese student, whom he recognized as also engaged in graduate work in the university. Mr. Balfour was introduced in due time and went through with his lecture. It was just such a masterly presentation as anyone would have anticipated from that speaker of the different ties that bind together the peoples of the world, common knowledge, common commercial interests, the intercourse of diplomatic relationship, and the bonds of human friendship. The speaker sat down amid a great outburst of applause. After the applause had died down, in the moment of silence when, after the Scotch fashion, the presiding officer had arisen to make his own little address of appreciation, Professor Lang said he saw this Japanese student stand up and lean over the balcony. Before the chairman could open his lips, the Japanese student had spoken. "But, Mr. Balfour," said he, "what about Jesus Christ?" Professor Lang said that one could have heard a pin drop in the hall. Everybody felt at once the justice of the rebuke. The leading statesman of the greatest Christian empire in the world had been dealing with the different ties that are to unite mankind and had omitted the one fundamental and essential bond. And everyone felt, too, the dramatic element in the situation, that the reminder of his forgetfulness had come to him from a Japanese student from a far-away non-Christian land. "But, Mr. Balfour, what about Jesus Christ?"

Now we are to answer the Japanese student's question. There is one great affirmation of St. Paul, which, in the field of thought with which Mr. Balfour was dealing. "The head of every man is Christ." In other words, the solution of the international problem is just the same as the solution of every problem, nothing else than Jesus Christ.

In St. Paul's great declaration, it seems to me we get right to the heart of the issue. Here he is setting forth the principle of human unity and the necessity to mankind of the instrumentalities through which its common life is to be expressed and by which its common work is to be done. He sets himself, of course, over against great and common opinions that govern the thought of many men in our day. We have been living for a good many years now under a conception of mechanistic nationalism, to which the idea of human unity is a very strange and alien thing, and as that rather hard and barren conception has been somewhat broken up in these last few years, it has been replaced by an equally noxious idea that applies the old evolutionary conceptions to human life in their very crudest form and conceives the history of the world to-day to be what it is alleged it has ever been, just one long, bitter jungle struggle for the survival of the fittest among the nations and the races and one unending conflict and rivalry among the environs for dominance and supremacy.

Of course, one cannot reconcile these theories with the actual facts of life, for there is no such struggle as this between the races and peoples, and there is no such bitter jungle rivalry as this dominating the spirit of mankind. It is good to offer against these notions that have control of modern, practical international politics, the far richer and truer conception of St. Paul. Little by little, we are making our way into the heart of that conception. We are beginning to realize the economic solidarity of mankind, that there is no such thing as a conflicting economic interest among the nations that does not mean in the end some common loss. We realize now that no nation permanently can gain if other nations permanently have to suffer as the compensation for its gain, that human trade must be balanced and compensatory, that we cannot make money out of other nations endlessly unless they make money also and equally out of us, that we are all bound together in one great economic body.

I remember how vividly the apprehension of this

came home to me just after the war had begun, when I had gone out in part to see what the effects of the war might be in the far-off ends of the earth. We were making our way through the jungles of central Siam. The British engineers had secured the concession to build a railway from Bangkok south through the whole spine of the Malay Peninsula to the cities of Penang and Singapore, and the German engineers had secured the concession to build the railway north from Bangkok to the frontiers of Yunnan in southern China. We were making our way up through the jungle and came at last to the railhead, where a little group of German engineers were still busy, Siam not having yet come in on the side of the Allies in the War. The German engineers were trying to master a river that ran right across the line of their northward advance. They had, of course, been getting their materials from home, just as the British engineers had done—that is where the profit of the concessions lay—and now there was, of course, no possibility of getting out any more building material from Germany and in bridging this new river the German engineers had to do the best they could with what they had on hand. It happened that down the line there was a bridge no longer needed over the stream for which it had been built. They brought that bridge up and inasmuch as it would not fit the northern river they changed the size of the river to fit the bridge. Far off there in the heart of the jungle, the German engineers were changing the topography of a Siamese river because of the necessities of the great struggle ten thousand miles away. We were buried in the heart of the great southeastern Asiatic jungles and yet we felt the tremors of that great strife, as though the guns had been thundering there along the waters of the Menam.

Little by little, I say, we are making our way into this conception that mankind has one common interest and that no part of mankind can gain without every other section of humanity profiting by that gain, nor any section of mankind suffer without all of us sharing in that suffering. And, of course, St. Paul's idea carries the conception much further than this solidarity of economic interest. He is conceiving of mankind as one great organic body embracing the whole human race, as an organism of which Jesus Christ is the head, with many members, all related integrally, one to another, all fulfilling their several parts and the whole body dependent upon the health and the freedom of each separate part and of its faithful activity and the subordination of the whole to its one rational and coördinating heart. We have the idea worked out in part in one of the greatest books of our generation, Mr. Thomas Hardy's *The Dynasts.* As Hardy sees Europe as one great organism, so the whole of human life is to be seen as one great biological unity, through which one common life is beating, governed by one common principle, animated or to be animated by one common dominant spirit.

St. Paul, I say, in reply to our Japanese student's question in McEwen Hall to Mr. Balfour, lays down for us the principle of human unity, which is Jesus Christ, and by the same token he lays down the method and the power of it. A Japanese friend, who was for some time in the Yokohama Specie Bank in New York—he happens to be a Japanese nobleman whom one cannot annoy more readily than by applying his titles to him—

wrote me of his experience in New York one Sunday when he had gone into the Broadway Tabernacle church to hear Dr. Jefferson preach. He said that when he went in, this whole problem of international relations was still a mystery to him, but when he came out it was as clear as the light of noonday. He realized in view of what he heard that morning that there is a solution to this problem and a perfectly clear and simple solution. It is simply that all the nations should submit themselves to the lordship of Jesus Christ. He said that he realized now that the problem of international relationships is not an insoluble one, but that we can achieve a human unity if we can unite every nation by itself first of all with Christ.

I remember years ago in the old town hall in Paisley, on the west coast of Scotland, hearing the late Dr. A. B. Wann put the principle in much the same way as my Japanese friend put it, saying that it was a mathematical axiom that if people will move toward one common point, they must move toward one another, and if they reach that common point, they will have reached a common association and fellowship, and that if all the nations of the world will press in toward the one great centre of the life of humanity, it must follow of necessity that all these peoples of the world will find themselves in a common company round about their one head and Lord.

So I might begin and end just here in our consideration of this question of Christianity and international relationships. The head of every man, that is the head of humanity, is Christ. And all that is necessary is just that humanity should recognize the realities, that it should adjust itself to the ultimate spiritual fact, that we should accept Jesus Christ, who is our head, and in the recognition of what we are, that is one great body to be governed by His spirit and mind, we should find the solution of all this chaotic discord of our day.

But this would be going quite too fast, and I presume we should go back over our ground a bit and try to analyze our problem more particularly. I should like to lay down what I have to say in four very simple statements.

The first is that a just and secure international order requires as essential to it some basis of agreement, and Christianity alone can adequately supply that basis. One of the strongest arguments against the League of Nations to-day is that the basis of moral concord underlying all the heterogeneous elements that enter into that association is not adequate. Many of those who have antagonized the League honestly I think have done so on this ground. They are convinced that the nation cannot unite except on some firmer and broader basis of common moral and intellectual concord.

Of course, that was just the difficulty which our American nation confronted at the beginning. I have been back to my old home in central Pennsylvania, where five generations of our family lie buried, running back to the Scotch-Irish Puritans long before the days of the Revolutionary War. The first of the long line was the first burgess of the town, Benjamin Elliott. He was sent by his constituents to the convention at Philadelphia, which was to determine whether Pennsylvania would accept the Constitution designed to establish the American nation. His constituents were opposed to Pennsylvania's accepting the proposed Constitution. "What," they argued, "ally ourselves with

Rhode Island! We have nothing ethically in common with that petty and repudiating State and we are resolved not to bind ourselves, our great commonwealth to other sections of totally different character and ideas.'' And when he came back from the convention, having voted that Pennsylvania should join with Rhode Island and the rest of the colonies in setting up the American nation, he was roughly handled by his constituents, who did not believe that there was an adequate basis of common moral agreement on which to launch this venture of the united American nation. Now it has turned out that there was an adequate basis of moral and intellectual concord. For my part, I believe that we have also an adequate basis among the nations of the world to justify the establishment of the League of Nations, that there is enough there of longing, of desire, of discontent, of revolt against the old order, enough there of positive purpose and view to furnish a basis of agreement on which to begin. But there is a measure of truth with those who still object. There will not be enough basis of agreement to last very long unless that foundation is to become broader.

There is an interesting passage in one of Sir Alfred Lyall's volumes, entitled *Asiatic Studies,* in which, surveying the history of the Asiatic states, he tries to determine what the function of religion has been in holding together a society of very diverse and heterogeneous elements, and his conclusion is that ''religion and intermarriage are the bonds that amalgamate or isolate sound groups'' and that ''religion has often shown itself more effective as a bond of union, than territorial patriotism.'' We know very well that it was only because Christianity at last supplied common religious sentiments and convictions to the vast, disintegrating Roman Empire that that empire was held together for still longer generations. Let me cite the fact in a paragraph from Professor Ramsay's *Pauline and Other Studies.*

In the minds of the ancients, no union of men, small or great, good or bad, humble or honorable, was conceivable without a religious bond to hold it together. The Roman Empire if it was to become an organic unity, must derive its vitality and its hold on men's minds, from some religious bond. Patriotism to the ancients was adherence to a common religion, just as the family tie was not common blood but communion in the family religion. Accordingly, when Augustus essayed the great task of consolidating the loosely aggregated parts of the vast Empire, he had to find a religion to consecrate the unity by a common idea and sentiment. The existing religions were all national, while the Empire was striving to extirpate the national divisions and create a supra-national unity. A new religion was needed. Partly with conscious intention, partly borne on the tide of events, the young Empire created the imperial religion, the worship of an idea,—the cult of the majesty of Rome as represented by the incarnate deity present on earth in the person of the reigning Emperor and by the dead gods, his deified predecessors on the throne. [Just exactly this Japan has tried to do in our generation.]

Except for the slavish adulation of the living Emperor, the idea was not devoid of nobility, but it was incapable of life because it degraded human nature and was founded upon a lie. But Paul gave the Empire a more serviceable idea. He made possible that unity at which the imperial policy was aiming. The true path of development for the Empire lay in allowing free play to the idea which Paul offered and strengthening itself through this unifying religion. That principle of perfect religious freedom, which we regard as Seneca's, directed for a time the imperial policy and caused the acquittal of Paul on his first trial in Rome. But freedom was soon exchanged for the policy of fire and sword. The imperial gods would not give place to a more real religion and fought for two and a half centuries to maintain their sham worship against it. When at last the idea of Paul was even reluctantly and imperfectly accepted by the emperors, no longer claiming to be gods, it gave new life to the rapidly perishing organization of the empire and conquered the triumphant barbarian enemy. If it had not been for Paul, if one may guess at what might have been, no man would now remember the Roman and Greek civilization. Barbarism proved too powerful for the Graeco-Roman civilization unaided by the new religious bond, and every channel through which that civilization was preserved or interest in it maintained, either is now or has been in some essential part of its course Christian after the Pauline form.

I believe that exactly what Christianity did for the Roman Empire in unifying its discord and giving it a basis on which its life could be prolonged, Christianity has to do for the nations to-day, and we shall never solve our international problems until we have provided human life with those religious conceptions by which alone mankind can be united against all that rends humanity asunder.

We should also remind ourselves that a just and secure international order is itself an idea which can only be kept alive by and upon other ideas adequate to sustain it and that only Christianity embodies and can supply those great ideas. I mean such ideas as, first, the idea of one God and one law. We are never going to bind together mankind in one just and secure international order if east and west of Suez there are different decalogues, if the same law does not run all the world around. We can never set up a unified humanity on any basis of polytheism or polynomism. There must be one head over all the great body and one great law laid down for all its life.

I mean, in the second place, such an idea as the moral and biological unity of humanity and the nonexistence of racial superiorities, except as conceived as superiorities of capacity to serve the whole. We cannot set up a satisfying and enduring international order save as we rest on the principle that God has actually made of one blood all the nations of men, and that what we are accustomed to speak of as racial superiorities are discriminations springing subjectively out of the preferences of the race that is doing the judging. As a matter of fact we ought to have a sense of proportion and perspective enough to realize as an historic fact and as a sociological fact to-day that every race thinks itself to be superior to other races.

I came the other day on an old book, Jedediah Morse's *American Universal Geography,* published in Boston in the year 1796, and I found in it this footnote. It was the story of an interview between an Indian chief and Colonel Morgan in 1766 at a great salt lick in Ohio. The old chief was a man of eighty-four, leading a band of Iroquois and Wyandotte Indians, and this was the tale he told Colonel Morgan:

> After the Great Spirit formed the world, He made the various birds and beasts which now inhabit it. He also made man but having formed him white and very imperfect and ill-tempered, he placed him on one side of the world, which he now inhabits, from which he has lately found a passage across the water to be a plague to us. As the Great Spirit was not pleased with this, His first work, he took black clay and made

what you call a negro, with woolly hair. This black man was much better than the white man but still he did not answer the wish of the Great Spirit; that is, he was imperfect. At last the Great Spirit, having procured a piece of pure red clay, formed from it the red man perfectly to his own mind, and He was so well pleased with him that He placed him on this great island separate from the white and black men, and gave him rules for his conduct, promising happiness in proportion as that should be deserved.

Now, that is the ingenious, instinctive judgment of each race upon the other. A friend of mine was traveling in the interior of China. He had lived there many years and was dressed as a Chinese and spoke the language as the people around him spoke it. He passed through a little town where there was a Christian church. As he went by the church and looked in, there was service going on and he stopped near the door to listen to what the Chinese preacher might be saying. He was setting forth his ideas of ethnology and explaining to his hearers that there were many different kinds and colors of people in the world. He said: "First of all, there are the white people, then there are the black people, then there are the red people, then there are the brown people, and then there are we Chinese, the skin colored people."

Every race thinks it is skin-colored and that the others are the tinted races of the world. We are never going to build a human order on such ideas. We have to realize that there is no inherently superior race. No doubt the so-called white race has many advantages and holds in trust much for other races which it is to share with them but every race has its qualities of superiority and I suppose that, if literally we were to judge races by the moral standards of the gospels, the negro race has more of those ethical, temperamental qualities which our Lord Jesus Christ exalted than any other race in the world. The superiority of which we feel conscious in the races is meaningless unless interpreted in terms of trusteeship for a united humanity.

In the third place, there is the idea of religious liberty, of the perfect freedom of the human spirit, without which we can never build a secure and just international order. We cannot build a united human order on any limitations of the freedom of the human spirit. We have to build it on the largest conceivable liberty and only Christianity has the conception of that type of liberty.

The kind of human order in which Christianity teaches us to believe requires a basis of universal human good will as well as common ideas. We are confronting to-day a very interesting new interpretation that bids fair to push off the ground the old conception of economic determinism, which had so much to do with landing us in this Hell that we are trying to get out of now in the world. We are replacing these old notions of economic necessitarianism with new ideas of climatic determinism. In his book, *The Conflict of Colour,* Mr. Putnam Weale sets forth the thesis that religious ideas, social conceptions, and political institutions are a matter of longitude and latitude, that they are determined by the climatic conditions which surround the people possessing these different ideas and institutions, that you cannot transport them from one climate to another. The theory of one common body of moral conceptions, of one common universal religion, he holds to be forbidden by the climatic diversities of the world.

Over against any such conclusions we just set our own human instinct of the unity of mankind, our conscious experience of brotherhood with men of every race, of every color, of every climate, of every section of the world. We have had enough of this experience of communicable religion, of interracial identity of spirit, of Christian understanding and acceptability to justify our conviction in this regard.

Let me cite three bits of testimony. The first one is from Mr. Fukuzawa, the most powerful nonofficial person in his day in Japan, the founder of the newspaper in Japan historically most nearly filling the position of the London *Times,* a man who has left his imprint deeply upon the educational, the intellectual, and the moral life of his land.

> There can be no doubt that many serious troubles would have occurred had not the Christian missionary not only shown to the Japanese the altruistic side of the occidental character, but also by his teaching and by his preaching imparted a new and attractive aspect to the intercourse, which otherwise would have been masterful and repellent. The Japanese cannot thank the missionary too much for the admirable leaven which he introduced into their relations with foreigners. . . . I once said that if no missionaries had ever come to our country, the dissoluteness and wantonness of foreigners would have come to be much greater and our relations to foreigners would not be what they are now.

Let me take another testimony from a far other land, from Sir William Wadsworth Young, coming back from his lieutenant-governorship of the Punjab in India and reporting to a great gathering of business men in St. Michael's in Cornhill in London.

As a business man speaking to business men, I am prepared to say that the work which has been done by missionary agency in India exceeds in importance all that has been done—and much has been done—by the British Government in India since its commencement. Let me take the province which I know best. I ask myself, what has been the most potent influence which has been working among the people since annexation fifty-four years ago? And to that question I feel there is but one answer, Christianity as set forth in the lives and teaching of Christian missionaries. I do not underestimate the forces which have been brought to bear on the races in the Punjab by our beneficent rule, by British justice and enlightment, but I am convinced that the effect on native character produced by the self-denying labors of missionaries is vastly greater. The Punjab bears on its historic roll the names of many Christian statesmen, men who have honored God by their lives and endeared themselves to the people by their faithful work. But I venture to say, if they could speak to us from the Great Unseen, there is not one of them who would not say that the work done by men like French and Clark and Newton and Forman, who went in and out among the people for a whole generation or more, who preached by their lives the nobility of self-sacrifice, and the love of God and man is a higher and nobler work, and more far-reaching in its consequences.

I offer one more testimony from a still different land, a long petition signed by Persian seals and Persian names from all the leading men of Kumanshah in southwestern Kurdish Persia, beginning with the Iman Jumeh, that is, the chief Mohammedan ecclesiastic of the city, followed by all the other leading Mohammedan ecclesiastics, the leading merchants and business men and bankers of the city. It is addressed to the Presbyterian Board of Foreign Missions, and it is an appeal that they will not take a certain medical missionary, Dr. Packard, away from that purely Mohammedan and Kurdish city because he and the new things he has brought are indispensable to the city.

I could multiply the evidence from all over the world. There are no climatic divisions that split mankind into irrevocable and incommunicable diversities that can never be unified. Human love leaps all boundaries. There is a fellowship that is of all mankind. We shall set up no satisfying international order unless we build it on foundations of universal human good will, and these only Christ can produce.

Last of all, the only kind of an international order that will endure, that will stand the strain which will surely come upon it, must be an order founded upon righteousness. No idea or institution that is not based on truth, and pervaded with truth, can enduringly prevail. And the kind of an order to whose realization we are working our way—so slowly—is an order that must rest on righteousness. Until we build the life of the world, all our international and interracial relationships, on the same foundation on which alone we can build our lives, we shall have no order of mankind, healing the discords, bridging the gulfs, relating men in one orderly universal human society.

I know how far away we are from this, but we are making progress across the years. Consider the principles that built up the British Empire in India and then compare them and the attitude of the conquering nation and of all the other nations of the world toward that process, with the principles on which the Congo Free State was founded, and mark the long progress in the interval. Then take the mandates under which the

German colonies are held now under the League of Nations by the different trustee nations to whom they are confided and compare the terms of those mandates with the principles on which the Congo Free State was built up. No one who will do this can deny that we have come a long, long way across the last hundred years toward bringing home to the consciousness of the world the sanctions of Christian duty and obligation and relationship.

But it may be that some will say: "Yes, but the task is too big for the forces on which you propose to lay it. Christianity has done about as much as anything has done, perhaps as much as could be hoped for, but the weight of the moral inertia of humanity, the deepest, inherent traditions that we brought up with us out of the jungle and that we cannot shake ourselves free from, the wolf nature in us that is as powerful and ravenous to-day as it ever was,—all these make a burden too heavy for Christianity even to bear." No, they do not. When one thinks of what has been achieved by a few scattered individuals operating in the spirit of Christ and toward His great goals, one does not despair of the absolute transformation of the world, if once for all the forces of humanity are laid open to the uses of Christ.

I can think back over this whole missionary generation, to the beginning of the Student Volunteer Movement, when it chose its bold motto, "The Evangelization of the World in This Generation." That generation has come to an end and the world has not been evangelized—but it might have been. It was not the fault of the ideal, it was only that the number of men and women, ready to forget everything else and lend themselves to the one supreme task for which Christ died, were not enough to enable God to reach the whole, big, moving mass of human life and cleanse it and lift it to the order that is His will for man. But some day it will come, because the head of every man—that is, the head of humanity—is Christ.